CALCUTTA REVISITED

EXPLORING CALCUTTA
THROUGH ITS BACKSTREETS AND BYWAYS

by
KEITH HUMPHREY

Grosvenor House
Publishing Limited

All rights reserved
Copyright © Keith Humphrey, 2014

The right of Keith Humphrey to be identified as the author of this
work has been asserted by him in accordance with Section 78
of the Copyright, Designs and Patents Act 1988

The book cover picture is copyright to Keith Humphrey
Cover illustrations: Rickshaws in Giri Babu Lane and Baithakhanna Lane

This book is published by
Grosvenor House Publishing Ltd
28-30 High Street, Guildford, Surrey, GU1 3EL.
www.grosvenorhousepublishing.co.uk

This book is sold subject to the conditions that it shall not, by way of
trade or otherwise, be lent, resold, hired out or otherwise circulated
without the author's or publisher's prior consent in any form of binding or
cover other than that in which it is published and
without a similar condition including this condition being imposed
on the subsequent purchaser.

A CIP record for this book
is available from the British Library

ISBN 978-1-78148-877-5

Also by Keith Humphrey

Walking Calcutta
ISBN 978-1-907211-04-1

Published by Grosvenor House Publishing
2009

All royalties from the author's books on Calcutta are donated to the Calcutta based NGO 'Calcutta Rescue' who undertake valuable work among the underprivileged of the City by providing a free comprehensive medical and health awareness service and educational and vocational programmes.

'The red lights did not forbid.
Yet the City of Calcutta stopped suddenly
In its tempestuous rush;
Taxis and private cars, vans and tiger crested
Double decker buses;
Stopped precariously in their tracks.
Those who came running and screaming
From both sides of the road
Porters, vendors, shopkeepers and clients;
Even now they are like still life;
On the artist's canvas.
Stunned they watch
Crossing from one side of the road;
To the other, with uncertain steps;
A child, completely naked.
It had rained in Chowringhee a short
while ago;
Now the sunlight has pierced the heart
Of the clouds
And is descending like an overlong shaft;
Calcutta shines with an eerie glow
I sit next to the bus window;
And look at the sky and you;
The child of a beggar mother;
Jesus of Calcutta..............'

From 'Jesus of Calcutta' (Kolkatar Jishu)
By Narendranath Chakraborty

Contents

	Page
Acknowledgements	1
Author's Note	2
Introduction	4

Chapter 1:
Finding your way around Calcutta — 15

Chapter 2:
Getting about in Calcutta — 17

Chapter 3:
Mahatma Gandhi Road to Colotola Street — 25

Chapter 4:
Colotola Street to BB Ganguly Street — 30

Chapter 5:
Colotola Street to Giri Babu Lane — 38

Chapter 6:
Mechua Bazar — 43

Chapter 7:
Mechua Fruit Market — 47

Chapter 8:
Armenian Street to Writers' Building — 51

Chapter 9:
In and around Dalhousie Square   57

Chapter 10:
Sonagachi   66

Chapter 11:
Ram Bagan   73

Chapter 12:
Pathuiriaghat   79

Chapter 13:
Nimtola Ghat   85

Chapter 14:
South East of BB Ganguly Street   90

Chapter 15:
Kumatoli and Sovabazar   94

Chapter 16:
Baghbazar (East)   108

Chapter 17:
Baghbazar (West)   113

Chapter 18:
College Street (Boi Para)   118

Chapter 19:
Baithakkhana   124

Chapter 20:
Bow Bazar (North   129

Chapter 21:
Bow Bazar (South)   135

CONTENTS

Chapter 22:
Raja Bazar (North)   140

Chapter 23:
Raja Bazar (South)   145

Chapter 24:
Burra Bazar (North)   150

Chapter 25:
Burra Bazar (South)   155

Chapter 26:
The Howrah Bridge and Howrah Station   161

Chapter 27:
South Park Street Cemetery   173

Chapter 28:
Calcutta in a day   185

Chapter 29:
Calcutta's markets   191

Chapter 30:
Other places of interest   194

Glossary   207

Old and New Street Names   212

Index   219

List of Illustrations

Plate 1	Howrah Bridge	100
Plate 2	Mullick Ghat Flower Market	100
Plate 3	Rabindra Sarani/Colotolla Street Crossing	101
Plate 4	Hari Ram Goenka Street	101
Plate 5	Bow Bazar, BB Ganguly Street	102
Plate 6	Royd Street/Elliot Road Crossing	102
Plate 7	Sun Yat Sen Street	103
Plate 8	Nirmal Chandra Street	103
Plate 9	Lal Dighi and Central Post Office	104
Plate 10	MG Road	104
Plate 11	Dharmatala Street	105
Plate 12	Knifegrinder in Baithakkhana Lane	105
Plate 13	Zakaria Street	106
Plate 14	Bow Bazar, by Sealdah Flyover	106
Plate 15	MG Road/Chiteranjan Avenue Crossing	107
Plate 16	Victoria Memorial Hall	107

All photographic images included in this book and cover are copyright of the author

*To the people of Calcutta
the unsung eighth wonder of the world
for their many kindnesses to me*

ACKNOWLEDGEMENTS

All that is in this book derives from my own first hand observations in Calcutta. As with my earlier book on the City, the methodology employed involved solitary extended stays in simple lodgings in one or other of the more densely populated quarters of the City and daily forays through the backstreets and byways of each of the areas being covered. In the tumultuous and pullulating metropolis which is Calcutta, this can be draining both physically and motivationally. I am therefore greatly indebted to all those who in their different ways helped keep my spirits raised sufficiently to enable me to complete my task. There were the various staff at my 'hotel' whose unrelenting inquisitiveness about my personal circumstances provided an endless source of amusement. The local pavement dwellers, hawkers and other street people remembered from previous visits, who never failed in having a friendly smile for me whenever I encountered them. Then there were the countless and nameless passers by who, the minute my notebook appeared, would stop and engage me in conversation and, having satisfied their curiosity, invariably wished me well.

I am also indebted once again to Chris Smy for his technical and design skills in reproducing my photographic images both within the book and those appearing on the covers.

My biggest debt however, is to my dear Bengali friend and Calcutta resident, Udita Chatterjee for her unfailing assistance in checking the many and various issues I raised with her and for being generous enough to spend her free time in my company on my rare rest days.

Author's Note

It is now five years since publication of 'Walking Calcutta' my original book for travellers to the City which until then, had been largely ignored by travel writers from the West. Ordinarily this would be the time for a review and update followed by publication of a revised edition.

That accepted, there is also a need to acknowledge and respond to the valuable feedback I have received since publication of Walking Calcutta. This feedback, from travellers kind and brave enough to have put their trust in me to guide them through the previously less explored quarters of the City had persuaded me that what was called for was something more than a simple revision of what had gone before.

Perhaps the overriding consideration is that for so many travellers, the vast majority in fact, their stay in Calcutta is of only short duration; far too limited to allow for undertaking the lengthy walking tours set out in my earlier book. The plea has been for shorter, less arduous and time consuming forays into more concentrated areas of interest. This book is my response.

I have endeavoured wherever possible, to explore Calcutta via its backstreets and byways, where most of daily life is lived. Those who wish to follow my routes need to be aware of just how unusual will be their presence in most of these localities. They can expect to be met with much good natured curiosity from locals and it is my hope that they will find this as rewarding to them as it always has been to me.

AUTHOR'S NOTE

Readers of my previous book will identify some repetition; something largely unavoidable in works involving so much factual observation. I have tried wherever possible to limit such repetition without discarding that which will be of enduring interest to the inquisitive traveller or advice useful to them. I hope that I have gone some way to achieving this.

As was my intention in writing Walking Calcutta, if this book can go some way in encouraging the traveller to see and experience Calcutta in a way they would not otherwise have been able to, then it will have achieved its purpose.

Calcutta has always been a very special place for me, indeed I believe there to be nowhere else on earth quite like it. The City and its people hold a singular place in my affections, unabated in more than forty years. This has drawn me back repeatedly over the years and I am sure it will continue to do so until the day I die.

In 2001, Calcutta officially renamed itself Kolkata which is more in line with the Bengali pronunciation. In this book I have stuck with Calcutta; not in any attitude of wilful defiance but simply because it seems more appropriate given the many historical references I have included.

Similarly, I have liberally employed the old names of many of the City's thoroughfares since officially renamed. I have taken this freedom wherever, in my experience, the original name is still in wider use locally than the new. The same applies with my spellings of thoroughfares and features where alternative and sometimes multiple, versions are in use; I have used the spellings I believe most widely employed. My objective has been to try to avoid confusion for those less familiar with the City. I hope the more knowledgeable will understand and allow me this indulgence.

Keith Humphrey
Suffolk, August 2014

Introduction

Preconceptions

There will be few travellers from the West, or elsewhere for that matter, who will travel to Calcutta free from preconceptions about the place; often of a highly negative nature. They will have heard often fearful accounts of a City in which rumour and hearsay suggests, there exists an urban awfulness on a monumental scale.

It is Calcutta's misfortune that the City has become a kind of metaphor for the extremes of squalor, deprivation, want and every other facet of human degradation. Few commentators, unless locals, have ever found anything nice to say about Calcutta. Rudyard Kipling seemingly loathed the City and there have been very many since who have shared his disapprobation.

From the 1960's a succession of film makers, writers and other commentators were drawn to Calcutta. With some notable exceptions, many came looking for what the Bengali writer Krishna Dutta so succinctly described as 'images of horror.' They found them in abundance and relayed these to their, mainly, Western audiences who of course, were not conditioned to reconcile what was being presented to them with their own existence in a developed and relatively affluent society. This was the beginning of a growing mass awareness of the work of Mother Theresa and her Missionaries of Charity amongst the City's poorest of the poor. If there was something positive resulting from all this intrusion it was the raising of the profile

INTRODUCTION

of the Missionaries' work, pricking Western consciences and leading to an increasing flow of donations.

What infuriated Indians generally and Bengalis particularly was what they saw as the complete lack of balance shown by these commentators. They were seen as being fixated solely upon the human degradation of Calcutta's slums, pavements and leper colonies with scant regard to either social or historical perspective or to the more positive aspects of the City. Reportage is one thing, ran the argument but why was it necessary to have lingering camera shots upon the faces of the dying destitutes at Nirmal Hriday (Mother Theresa's house for the dying), or footage of animals wallowing in the filth of open sewers juxtaposed with scenes of children playing?

Whatever the arguments, the legacy of all this was to reinforce an already negative image of Calcutta as a place of squalor and human degradation on a massive scale; somewhere very nasty indeed where rumour would have you believe that the destitiute and leprous lay dying in gutters around every street corner.

Whilst anyone who knows Calcutta would dismiss this most extreme view as absurd, it is not entirely without foundation. Calcutta in its worst aspects can be a frightening and terrible place. It can also be a place of great warmth with a strong artistic, literary and culinary culture. All Calcutta will ask is that you come with an open mind and form a judgement from your own first-hand experience.

On being a Pedestrian in Calcutta

You achieve a better understanding of any city if you are prepared to walk its highways and byways. You travel more slowly so have better opportunity to observe more of both the good and the bad. More importantly is that in walking you are in closer proximity with the city's populace; they are more accessible to you as you are to them. Nowhere can this be more rewarding than in teeming Calcutta.

Walking as the preferred means of exploration will not readily be understood by locals. They will ask you why you don't hire a car and driver or at least take a taxi. Your, to them, odd behaviour will do much to reinforce their view of foreigners as being eccentric characters.

The main considerations for the pedestrian in Calcutta are climate, traffic and what lies underfoot.

The climate in Calcutta, situated as it is on what was once swampland and salt marsh astride the Tropic of Cancer can make for a punishing environment.

The winter months from October to February provide weather that is mainly dry and relatively cool. This is when many of the locals are to be seen walking about swathed in blankets and winter headgear and where street corner bonfires are not unknown. My friend Udita would often appear at such times in heavy cardigan, scarf, woolly hat and even gloves.

The summer months from around March to May/June are seriously hot with temperatures rarely below 36C and often as high as 43/44C. Added to this is either suffocatingly high humidity levels or the 'loo', a furnace like, dry shrivelling wind.

The summer months are followed by the Monsoon, generally from June/July to September. During these months there will be occasions when many streets in central and north Calcutta will be awash with rainwater; where motorised traffic and trams cannot move, only the hardy rickshaw pullers who are then kings of the road.

Traffic considerations for the pedestrian are twofold. Pollution levels are very high; you can actually experience that metallic

INTRODUCTION

taste in your mouth at certain times of the day. There is just no avoiding it.

Of more immediate concern is the aggressiveness of Calcutta's traffic. I used to believe that this was only surpassed by that found in lawless Patna in the neighbouring State of Bihar. No longer; Calcutta has now taken over this dubious distinction. There is a clear hierarchy based on size. Trams, heavy lorries and buses are at the top and you, the vulnerable pedestrian, are definitely at the bottom; below even the long suffering rickshaw puller.

When crossing any road, never assume that anything on wheels from a bicycle to a tram, will give way to you. It will not. Such a gesture would not even be understood; the philosophy is 'you are in my way so you must take your chances'. That the pedestrian may be elderly, infirm or even blind, will make no difference; no hint of consideration will be given.

In the main thoroughfares use only the controlled crossings (manned mainly by the excellent white uniformed Traffic Police often assisted by volunteer students). If in any doubt, follow the locals who, of necessity, have developed highly tuned survival instincts.

Be particularly wary of the battered, blue and yellow painted passenger buses operated by private transport undertakings. These will stop suddenly almost anywhere to set down and pick up fares. They will move off with just as little regard and their drivers are notorious for being speed crazed risk takers. You will read almost daily, reports in the City's press of accidents, often resulting in fatalities, involving these vehicles. Such reports invariably conclude with the statement that the driver and conductor absconded: a wise move given the level of anger invoked in passengers and pedestrians by such incidents. Lynchings are not unknown.

A recent and unwelcome addition to this vehicular anarchy is the LPG powered motor rickshaw. These green and yellow painted pests seemingly double in number at my every visit to the City. The drivers are a law unto themselves, even by Calcutta's appalling driving standards and the sheer manoeuvrability of these vehicles makes them suddenly appear at great speed where they are least expected.

With few exceptions, the footpaths of Calcutta's thoroughfares are challenging to the pedestrian. In the main roads throughout the City there can be hardly ten consecutive metres of unobstructed or reasonably flat pavement on which to tread. You and fellow pedestrians will have to share the pavement with small traders, astrologers, catering enterprises, chai stalls, sleepers, badly parked vehicles, the occasional cow, goats, chickens, dogs, bathers at standpipes, ramshackle temporary settlements, madly placed lighting columns and advertising hoardings and the ever present but unexplained piles of rubble. All life is here, it is relentless, inescapable and a privilege to be amongst it all.

One further peculiarity of Calcutta is that almost every pavement appears to have been repeatedly excavated to lay or repair the service pipes and cables beneath but never properly reinstated. The result is that the excavations have either been under filled, providing a kind of zigzag, gully, often rain filled, or overfilled, creating a sort of meandering hump which, try as you might, you can never quite, successfully negotiate whilst maintaining a normal walking pattern.

On Street Names and Numbering

To the uninitiated, the naming of Calcutta's streets and the numbering of the buildings within them can be confusing, amusing and sometimes mildly frustrating

Since Independence, the Calcutta Municipal Corporation has engaged in the renaming of literally hundreds of the City's

INTRODUCTION

thoroughfares. It even maintains a standing Road Renaming Committee for this purpose. Often, the motive for renaming has been to introduce an Indian and remove an Imperial connection. Hence, Wellesley Street became Bidhan Sarani, Amherst Street, Raja Ram Mohan Road Charnock Place Netaji Subhas Road, and Harrison Road Mahatma Gandhi Road and so on. Interestingly, there have been some splendid omissions. Still lurking just south of Shakespeare Sarani (erstwhile the old Theatre Road), are some thoroughfares of blatantly imperialist connection, these being Victoria Terrace and Albert Road, each occupying a side of Victoria Square. In other cases, street names have been changed to honour respected and significant Indian and other personalities. For example, Chitpore Road became Rabindra Sarani, the Lower Circular Road, A.J. Chandra Bose Road, and Dharmatala Street, Lenin Sarani and so on. The list seems endless.

Sometimes these new names have caught on, sometimes they have not. Not all such renaming seems to have met with majority approval by the City's citizens. The result is that often you will find both the old and the new names in common usage, depending on who you are talking to or which map, guide or reference book you consult. For example, Dalhousie Square seems more widely used than the new name B.B.D. Bagh. Likewise, Chowringhee seems to enjoy wider usage than Jawaharlal Nehru Road as does Sealdah Flyover than Bidyapati Setu or Canning Street over Biplabi Rash Behari Bose Road. There are scores of similar examples of this dual usage, all seemingly designed to confound and bewilder the traveller intent on exploring Calcutta.

Where the Corporation's Road Renaming Committee has really excelled itself is where it has renamed only part of a continuous thoroughfare or has allocated different names to different stretches. Beadon Street, travelling west to east, is first Beadon Street, then Dani Ghosh Sarani, then back to Beadon

Street and, finally, Abhedananda Road It is much the same with Colotolla Street which becomes Maulana Saukat Ali Lane as it nears Chitteranjan Avenue and, east of this, Anagarika Dharmapala Street.

To help overcome potential confusion, a list of the old street names and their replacement new names is included towards the end of this book. This list is by no means exhaustive, being mainly restricted to the thoroughfares of those quarters of the City which I have covered. A more comprehensive list may be found in Calcutta Yellow Pages; an indication of how widespread is the confusion caused.

The provision of formal street nameplates in Calcutta can also be patchy. The older quarters of the City are the best signed but be prepared for the sign to read the old, rather than the new street name or to be spelt in some archaic form, for example, Mitter instead of Mitra.

Of enormous help to navigation is that nearly every shop or business, however small, includes the address on their signboard. Again, be prepared for inconsistencies. It is not at all uncommon to find adjoining premises where one will display the new street name and the other the old name. I recently watched a sign writer beautifully executing 'Lower Chitpore Road' on the signboard of a shop surrounded by other premises all bearing the street name 'Rabindra Sarani'. Equally helpful, particularly outside of commercial areas, is the widespread use of mail boxes affixed to most residential premises. These invariably show the family name, house number and street name. Incredibly, these sometimes show both the old and new street names. Hence, the mail box of the thoughtful Ghose family of Amar Bose Sarani reminds passers-by that this thoroughfare was once called, and is still known by many as, Chor Bagan Lane

Street numbering enjoys particular peculiarities for the traveller to grasp. First amongst these is that a street number can relate to the whole block in which a particular premises is situated. The block itself may contain very many individual premises which, to outward appearance all seem separate entities. So, when at first you are unable to find any trace of, say Chaudhuri Cosmetics Ltd at 207 Rabindra Sarani, the chances are that it is located down the adjoining side street which forms part of the same block which faces Rabindra Sarani. It will share the 207 Rabindra Sarani address, proudly displayed on the shop front name board but actually the premises is physically located half way down adjoining Burtollah (sometimes shown Bartala) Street It can take some getting used to.

Another difficulty is where there has been demolition which has fragmented once single continuous thoroughfares. This is often found where the old Calcutta Improvement Trust (CIT) had been active. A good example can be found in what remains of Calcutta's old central Chinatown to the north of B.B Ganguly Street between the Rabindra Sarani and Chitteranjan Avenue crossings. Here, you will find the ancient Blackburn Lane now scattered in three separate locations, following division by demolition and the laying out of India Exchange Place Extension and New C.I.T. Road. Here, as in other similarly affected locations, no renumbering seems to have taken place to compensate for the buildings cleared away.

On Personal Space and Privacy

From the moment the western traveller first sets foot in Calcutta all previously held concepts of privacy and personal space must be abandoned.

The traveller has come to one of the most densely populated cities on earth and, until departure, will have hardly a waking moment when not part of a throng or more than half an arm's length away from a fellow human being.

To illustrate this, the latest (2011) census data gives a population density per square kilometre of the area covered by the Calcutta

Municipal Corporation, of almost 25,000. This is an average figure; within some wards in the central and northern parts of the City, Muchipara for example, the density will be higher, in some cases approaching 32,000. By comparison the corresponding figures for New York and for London are 10,870 and 4,934 respectively. Even teeming Bombay (Mumbai), now the most populous city of the sub-continent, is less densely populated than Calcutta, with a corresponding figure in the order of 23,000.

Staggering though these figures are, there is more to it than mere numbers suggest. So much of life in Calcutta takes place on the streets, where you can have your hair cut, be shaved, have your fortune told, your washing, ironing and cooking done, eat, bathe and sleep if you wish to, that the notion of personal space sinks to irrelevance. You are perhaps only reminded of the notion when walking across the Maidan, possibly the only truly open space anywhere in Calcutta proper where you could confidently hurl a chapatti in any direction without fear of hitting someone.

Even on those very rare occasions when you may believe yourself to be alone, you seldom are in fact. There will be any number of times when, on sitting to take a rest in some relatively quiet backwater, you hear a disembodied 'hello' cast in your direction. It may take you some minutes to discover the source of this greeting, often found to be an open window, doorway or a balcony above where your unseen company has been loitering. If there is any corner of Calcutta where it is possible to be truly alone, then I have yet to find it.

Then there is the business of nosiness. Indians because they are such an intelligent people are also amongst the most unashamedly inquisitive and nowhere is this trait more pronounced than in Calcutta. There seems to be a positive

INTRODUCTION

virtue in knowing the business of others and of them knowing yours. Where they do not know your business, they will often make assumptions. The staff at my 'Hotel' became utterly convinced that the purpose of my friend Udita regularly calling round to see me was that we were negotiating marriage. My explanations that I already had a wife of long standing back in England and that Ms Chatterjee was half my age did nothing to dispel the situation they had collectively created for us and would no doubt embellish over time.

Indians are great observers who love involving themselves in your affairs, however fleetingly. You can hardly ever stop to consult a map, look at your watch or cast a sedulous eye over something without attracting at least a few curious passers-by. I was once sat near the Srimani Market up in north Calcutta, absorbed in writing up my notes. On looking up I discovered that, in the few minutes I had been sitting there, a small crowd of at least a dozen people had gathered around me, curious to see what this 'firanghee' was up to. There was even a kind of spokesman, relaying to those without such a good view, exactly what was going on.

All this inquisitiveness is conducted in the most polite and friendly manner and nor is it at all one-sided. Countless times I have been passing by some incident or mild altercation which, in true Calcutta fashion, I have stopped to observe. It is nearly always the case that one of your fellow observers will feel compelled to tell you what it is all about together with any relevant background to the incident or, if known, the respective characters of the parties involved.

Until the traveller adjusts, all this observation and inquisitiveness can breed feelings of mild paranoia in the less emotionally secure. So many times it will happen that the traveller returns, seemingly unobserved, to their lodgings or hotel room when, almost immediately there is a knock at the door. It will be your laundry, a message, a bill to sign. You saw no one on your return but 'they' knew you were back, indeed the very minute you were back. The first time my wife and I stayed at the old Great Eastern Hotel we would return to our room in the evenings through the labyrinthine, dimly lit and deserted corridors with not a soul in sight. But the minute we turned into our corridor and long before we gained our room, two and sometimes three smiling faces would appear from the room used by housekeeping staff at the far end of the passageway. We never once succeeded in reaching our room undetected. It became a kind of elaborate game, which, on reflection, we never had any chance of winning.

Chapter 1

FINDING YOUR WAY AROUND CALCUTTA

Once you get a few basic bearings, Calcutta's main thoroughfares are not difficult to navigate. For our purposes the main north/south artery is Chitteranjan (CR) Avenue and its northern extension Jantindra Mohan (JM) Avenue. Parallel, to the west, is Rabindra Sarani (the old Chitpore Road), then the River Hooghly. To the east of CR Avenue and running roughly parallel to it, is Nirmal Chandra Street which as it progresses north, becomes College Street then Bidhan Sarani. Further east lies the Circular Road. These four main north/south routes are crossed east to west by (starting in the south) BB Ganguly Street, Mahatma Gandhi (MG) Road, Vivekananda Road, Arabinda Sarani, Baghbazar Street and the Circular Canal.

Between this rough grid of main thoroughfares it is a very different matter altogether. Here, crammed tightly with pullulating side streets and crisscrossed by narrow winding lanes are the areas which this book explores.

After a lot of thought I decided against including maps for a number of reasons. Many of the more detailed maps of

Calcutta contain significant inaccuracies. Even those provided by the major web browsers whilst generally accurate in their schematic layout, can contain serious errors; mainly by placing named streets in incorrect locations thereby rendering questionable their usefulness as an aid to navigation. Another consideration was that to provide clear maps depicting many of the tiny backstreets and byways with which this book deals would mean they would have to be on a very large scale. This would have rendered the book both unwieldy and unnecessarily expensive to the reader.

Perhaps the most reliable and accurate maps available are those of the Calcutta Police which may be viewed on their official website www.kolkatapolice.org. There is a separate map for each of the City's Police Districts. Unfortunately, I have never been able to gain consent for reproducing these maps either in full or part.

I have therefore paid particular attention to the detailed directions set out in each chapter, giving a prominent start and end location wherever possible. Using these directions, travellers should have no difficulty in navigating the various areas described.

Chapter 2

GETTING ABOUT IN CALCUTTA

Calcutta is arguably, one of the easiest of the major cities of the sub-continent in which to get yourself about. Generally, public transport fares are very inexpensive. Probably your only difficulty will be accumulating sufficient small change to fund your tickets.

The Metro

With the coming of the Metro system in the early 1970's (the first in India), the City enjoyed a fast, traffic free means of transport along Calcutta's north/south spine. Since those early days, the system has been considerably improved and extended. From Dum Dum in the north the service extends southwards beyond Tollygunge to Kavi Nazrul with a further extension south towards New Garia, currently under construction. Approval has also been given for Metro line 2 which will run from Rajarhat in the east, through Salt Lake to Sealdah then via Dalhousie Square, under the River Hooghly to Howrah Railway station and on westwards to New Dasanager in Howrah District. Other extensions linking to Calcutta International Airport are on the drawing board.

The Metro system like its counterparts in other major cities across the world, can become very congested at peak travel times. But it is a clean and very efficient means of moving rapidly about the City. A journey from, say Rabindra Sadan, just beyond the junction of Chowringhee and the lower Circular Road, to Girish Park in North Calcutta, will take no more than fifteen minutes. The same journey by road would be anyone's guess given Calcutta's legendary traffic jams. In the last year or two many of the 'rakes' as the carriages are called have even been provided with air conditioning.

Fares are currently 5, 10 or 15 Rupees depending on distance. There are tokens instead of tickets which get you through the access barriers at the start of your journey and the exit barriers at your destination station.

The Circular Railway

The second arm of Calcutta's mass rapid transport system is the Circular Railway.

As the name implies, it follows a circular (actually an extended oval) route from Dum Dum in the north, south westwards following the line of the River Hooghly from Baghbazar to Khidepur before turning north east through Tollygunge, Ballygunge, Park Circus, Kankurgachi, Ultadanga then back to Dum Dum.

The Circular Railway provides a very useful service for longer journeys across the City, particularly its eastern arm which covers areas well distanced from the current Metro service. As with the Metro, the service can become extremely congested at peak travel times. There are plans to extend the line from Dum Dum to the International Airport.

Fares vary according to the distance travelled, generally in multiples of five rupees.

GETTING ABOUT IN CALCUTTA

Trams

Easily my favourite means of getting around Calcutta. I actually prefer the older type of Tram which is more open than the modern version.

These clanking, battered steel monsters are an iconic symbol of Calcutta and integral part of the City's heritage.

Routes have been reduced over the years but there is still an adequate service to cover the north/south routes from Baghbazar, Belgachia and Bidhan Nager in the north to Khidepur and Tollygunge in the south. At one time Trams ran across the Howrah Bridge but nowadays terminate at the eastern side of the Bridge.

There is a flat fare of five rupees. A full schedule of tram routes and distances can be found at:
www.calcuttatramways.com

Buses

Calcutta's complex system of State run and privately operated buses is something of a nightmare for the occasional visitor to the City. Most have their routes emblazoned on their battered sides, eg, Bidhan Nager to Howrah etc. However, sometimes this will be in Bengali script only. Unless you know the exact routes, some of which can be byzantine, you could be in for a mystery tour.

The major disadvantage with the buses is the same as all roads transport in Calcutta; the unpredictability of traffic flow, involving sometimes horrendous traffic jams. The buses are also for the most part, horribly crowded and since picking up and setting down points can be fairly arbitrary, entering or leaving them can be a risky business.

Bus fares are in bands according to distance travelled. The minimum fares are six rupees for minibuses, seven rupees for state buses and five rupees for privately operated (blue/yellow) buses

Full details of all private, state and minibus routes can be found at:
www.calcuttayellowpages.com/busroute.hmtl

Taxis

Calcutta's taxi drivers have become legendary, generally for all the wrong reasons. Their antics feature regularly in the letters columns of many of the City's daily newspapers: proof that the locals too can fall victim to their caprices, not just travellers from outside.

The traveller arriving by air will join the orderly queue at the Airport's pre-paid taxi counter. They would do well to check that the destination written on their receipt corresponds with that you told the clerks since the latter have a habit of simply entering 'Esplanade' or 'Dalhousie' or something else familiar to them. 'Sudder Street' is one their favourites, on the assumption that for a non Indian traveller, that is the place to go.

Armed with their receipt, amended appropriately, the traveller reports to the small Bidhan Nagar Police Department booth opposite the exit doors. Here, lists will be consulted and a cab number scribbled on your receipt. The traveller can then either locate the given taxi from the snaking line along the kerbside or, preferably use the services of one of the official or non official porters hanging about by the booth, to do this for you and load your bags.

GETTING ABOUT IN CALCUTTA

Now there are some very good and knowledgeable taxi drivers in Calcutta and luckily the majority of these seem to work the Airport run. There are others unfortunately, mainly Biharis and Oriyas from out of State whose navigational skills are somewhat limited. It is a good idea before setting off to ascertain if your driver knows how to get to your destination; giving the driver the chance to consult his colleagues or your porter in case of uncertainty.

I can usually tell within a few minutes from setting off if the driver really knows where he is going and, if not, then help him with directions. The more casual visitor to the City will not have this advantage.

Calcutta is one of those cities where you can hail a taxi in the street, unlike, say Hyderabad or Bangalore where you have to telephone. The process can be hit and miss. Getting a taxi to stop for you can be a problem and it is not uncommon for the driver to then refuse to take you where you want to go if this is in some way inconvenient to him. Theoretically, you can report him to the Police for this refusal but realistically, who has the time? Some taxi drivers will rely on their meter others will refuse to use it. So it is important to agree a fare before setting off. This will save any argument later, particularly if the driver's poor navigation makes for a longer journey than was anticipated.

The City's licensing body is trying to overcome some of the problems by encouraging an increase in 'fixed fare' and 'no refusal' taxis. These are normally painted white rather than the traditional yellow.

For all the negatives, there are still a lot of honest and helpful taxi drivers about and it is still a convenient means of getting about the City, traffic conditions allowing.

Rickshaws

Rickshaws fall into two categories; the motorised green and yellow contraptions and the hand pulled type, unique to Calcutta.

The motorised and LPG fuelled rickshaw is of fairly recent introduction to Calcutta. They are restricted to operating in quite rigidly defined areas which are indicated on the back of the vehicles. These rickshaws are intended for relatively short journeys only and, unless you request and pay for the privilege, the driver will pick up other fares en route. This is quite normal and is a rather good way of meeting locals.

As a pedestrian, the traveller can quickly come to hate the motorised rickshaws for their ability to obstruct your passage at every turn, particularly when crossing a road when they can suddenly appear from nowhere.

There has recently been much public concern at the proliferation of unlicensed motorised rickshaws and disregard by rogue drivers of traffic regulations.

The more benign hand pulled rickshaw is an iconic symbol of Calcutta, much to the chagrin of some State politicians who regard this as giving the City a negative and backward image. This has resulted from time to time in calls for and actual attempts to abolish this ancient form of transport.

Originally introduced in the closing decade of the 19th century by Chinese shopkeepers to ferry their goods around the City and, since 1919, permitted to carry passengers. There is still a significant use of these rickshaws in transporting goods; most of the daily newspapers are delivered to street corner newsvendors in this way.

Back in 2005, the State Government decided that the hand pulled rickshaw was no longer compatible with what they wished to be the City's image and therefore had to go. The difficulty of course was what was to happen to the estimated 35,000 or so rickshaw pullers who were economically dependent on this form of transport. The introduction of the LPG fuelled motorised rickshaw was seen as a way forward in the phasing out the hand pulled variety. Although the authorities have certainly tightened up on the licensing of the hand pulled rickshaws, one should not expect any early transformation. As with so much else in the City, the arguments will rage back and forth interminably before any definite change will come about.

I have only ever used the hand pulled rickshaw to transport luggage or purchases for me. I have never been able to feel comfortable with the idea of being pulled along by another human being. But such squeamishness certainly should not be allowed to get in the way of these noble chaps earning a living. You hail them as you would do a taxi. In the rains they are often the only transport running through the flooded streets. Agree a price with the puller before you set off.

River Ferries

Second only to the Trams, the river ferries are a favourite way of getting around, although clearly more limited in terms of the destinations served.

For our purposes we are concerned with the ferries which ply between Baghbazar Ghat in the north of the City and Howrah Ghat, adjacent to the Railway Station. After leaving Baghbazar Ghat the ferry calls first at Sovabazar Ghat, then Ahriatola Ghat before crossing to the other side of the River and docking at Howrah Ghat. The total journey time is approximately twenty minutes including stops and the flat fare is six and half

Rupees. There are small cubby hole ticket offices adjacent the boarding ramps at each ferry ghat. At Howrah Ghat there is a kind of small booking hall with different ticket windows for the various destinations written above each in faded lettering.

From Howrah other ferries run across the River to Chandpal and Babu Ghats on the eastern bank and from there, smaller ferries can take you back across the River to Shibpur and other destinations on the western bank.

Most of the ferries run at approximately 20 to 30 minute intervals. Travellers will need to retain their tickets which will need to be given up at their destination.

Chapter 3

Mahatma Gandhi Road to Colotolla Street

A good starting point for this walk (and one which will become familiar), is the south western corner of the junction of Mahatma Gandhi (MG) Road with Chitteranjan (CR) Avenue.

The nearest Metro station is MG Road, approximately 200 metres north of this point.

At peak time this is one of Calcutta's busiest junctions. Chitteranjan (CR or Central as it is widely known) Avenue is one of the main north/south arteries and MG Road the busiest east/west artery linking Calcutta's two main railway stations; Howrah and Sealdah.

Keeping to the southern pavement, head west along MG Road passing the Hotel White House on the right and a little further on, the Hotel Himalay on the left. Both these establishments have excellent vegetarian restaurants attached which are clean, comfortable and inexpensive.

Just before the Hotel Himalay, at the back edge of the pavement was the usual pitch of Mr Bishu Das, an elderly astrologer and palmist. Over the years he had become something of a friend who I sought out on my every visit to Calcutta. On my latest visit he was not there in his usual spot and no one seemed to know what had happened to him. Aware that he had health problems over the last few years and had become quite frail, I feared the worst. So often does this happen in Calcutta; someone who has been part of the street scene for years, suddenly vanishes and is never heard of again.

Just past the Hotel Himalay, is a well stocked liquor shop where, instead of the usual iron grills, you conduct your business through a postcard size cut out in the plate glass frontage.

The next turning on the left is Ram Lochan Mullick Street, unmistakable by the huge midden of rubbish being energetically cleared by diggers and trucks of the Calcutta Municipal Corporation (CMC). Most of this rubbish is dumped her daily from the vast Mechua Fruit Market, located just behind the northern frontage of MG Road.

The Street will also be jam packed with huge lorries, many being loaded or unloaded by an army of coolies (which in Calcutta is a perfectly respectful and appropriate term). The reason for this is that the surrounding streets are home to many trucking and haulage enterprises, transporting goods all over India. An examination of the licence plates will show just how far some of these trucks have come; from Tamil Nadu, Karnartaka and Rajastan, even Kashmir.

Weaving through all this mayhem and keeping over to the left, the street bends to the right before becoming N. Badruddin Street. Often when passing through this Street, the scene resembles some medieval battlefield. Pools of what looks like blood collecting all over the pavement and flowing into the gutters; eerily set off by a blanket of smoke hovering around knee height. Actually it is not blood but red dye being boiled in pots over charcoal burners outside the tiny workshops lining the western pavement.

It is worth a few minutes having a look what is involved. Men (for some reason it seems to be a male dominated occupation), armed with a variety of wooden pattern blocks are dabbing these in the dye then applying this to unrolled bales of cloth. Some will be creating various border designs on the cloth, others random patterns. The finished result gives a pattern which is so even and uniform it is indistinguishable from something created by sophisticated factory machines.

At the end of the Street a right turn brings you into Zakaria Street. This busy and vibrant thoroughfare links CR Avenue to the east with Rabindra Sarani (erstwhile Chitpore Road) to the west.

The western end of Zakaria Street is dominated by the towering, green domed Nakhoda Masjid (Mosque). The Mosque, whose domes and minarets rise to more than fifty metres above street level, contains a massive prayer hall which can accommodate up to ten thousand. Built in the 1920's, it is modelled on the mausoleum of the Mughal Emperor Akba at Secundra.

This section of Zakaria Street is packed with budget guest houses, hostels and lodges. The' Rajasthan', the 'National U.P', 'Hotel De Luxe' and many others. All are what may be termed 'basic', some deplorably so. Recommended only for the adventurous, desperate or impecunious.

Crossing over Zakaria Street from N. Baruddin Street, the first turning on the left opens out into Ismail Madan Lane. In this Lane, the scene is one of goats; scores of them, some tethered at the back edge of the pavement, others roaming freely or lounging all over the roadway. This is also the place for specialists in basic travel, particularly by bus to Dhaka, Chittagong and other points east.

At the end of the Lane, a right turn leads into Badal (often shown Bolai) Dutta Street where, over to the right is the grisly spectacle of a street butchers shop. This one seems to specialise in goat meat with heads, hooves and entrails being particularly prominent display lines. You will see the butchers cutting the meat against a large, lethal looking and razor sharp fixed blade. This is known as a Bonti which comes in various sizes and is in almost universal domestic and commercial use all over India for all kinds of food preparation.

The Street is home to the most amazing amount of recycling. There are enterprises stripping cable for the copper wire; flattening out metal binding from barrels and packing cases; unravelling steel cable and all manner of processes involving anything metallic.

Then there is the timber recycling. Pallets, packing cases and other containers made of wood are being carefully dismantled into their component parts, from thin strips of wood to sizeable planks. Nothing at all is wasted; even extracted nails are carefully set aside for later recycling. All this industry is very much concerned with the initial stages of recycling; the dismantling, grading and sorting of materials. The use to which all this be applied will be witnessed in the course of other forays set out elsewhere in this book.

The Street performs a ninety degree turn to the left just past a popular communal standpipe at which several bathers will be liberally soaping themselves before rinsing off the suds with upended buckets of water. Just about this point I have often seen a local lady making her way along the roadway on her haunches. Possibly in her early thirties she clearly has no use of her lower limbs; infantile paralysis from Polio perhaps. Although disadvantaged in this way, her mobility is quite amazing, often dragging a full shopping bag along with her. For the traveller from this west this is not a sight which will sit easily with them: there will be many more in the course of their exploration of Calcutta.

The short remainder of the Street contains more of the recycling enterprises seen earlier although here will be seen huge piles of the dismantled materials, stacked and awaiting collection.

The Street spills out into the northern side of Colotolla Street. This Street, one of the oldest trading streets in Calcutta, once ran uninterrupted all the way eastwards to College Street. Now thanks to the mania for street renaming, it becomes Maulana Saukat Ali Lane about 100 metres east and Anagarika Dharmapala Street after it crosses CR Avenue.

Turning right into Colotolla Street and 50 metres on is the junction with Rabindra Sarani. The view to the right is dominated by the towering form of the Nakhoda Mosque, beyond which is the junction with MG Road. From that junction it is a five minute walk eastwards to return to the starting point.

Chapter 4

COLOTOLLA STREET TO BIPIN BEHARI (BB) GANGULY STREET

The starting point for this walk is where the last walk ended: the junction of Colotolla Street with Rabindra Sarani, just south of the landmark Nakhoda Mosque.

The route lies east along Colotolla Street, taking the first turning on the right into Harin Bari Lane. The entrance to the Lane is narrow, not much more than a few metres wide and usually thronged with people. It needs care to locate.

The Lane, narrow and crowded, as is the onward route thereafter, runs roughly parallel to Rabindra Sarani which is never much more than 50 metres or so to the right. Here however, it is a different environment entirely.

On first entering the Lane, the senses are immediately assailed; the noise, the congestion and the smells, the smells particularly. It is a filthy place, even by local standards; made more insalubrious by the large number of butchers' shops spilling their offal all over the surface of the Lane. In wet weather it is truly atrocious underfoot.

The open fronted premises of these dealers in meat are festooned with the hanging carcases of goats, sheep chickens and other less easily identifiable creatures. There is even beef on sale here but never pork for this is an almost exclusively Muslim area.

Progressing down the Lane, one realises just how little of the carcases is wasted. There will be piles of whole goat skins stacked ready for collection by men on bicycles. For some reason it always seems to be bicycles although given the extreme narrowness of the byways hereabouts this is almost certainly the most efficient form of transport. It is still nevertheless unpleasant when one scrapes past you with its load of dripping skins.

There will be piles of goats' heads, legs and hooves being stripped down for who knows what end use. Cows' hooves are also here in abundance possibly destined for some back street glue factory. While taking in this visual feast, there will be barrows full of animal entrails trundling down the Lane past you; followed by street dogs eager for anything which slops out.

This being a Muslim area, there are many beggars along the Lane (Muslims having a religious duty to give alms to the poor). Many of these beggars will be blind or at least present themselves to be so, often accompanied by a sighted helper. There is one pair who are in evidence nearly every time I pass this way. One is an elderly legless man being pushed along on a homemade wooden trolley not much larger than a skateboard, by an equally aged, partially blind and lame male colleague. There is another here who does not have the advantage of a helper and who shunts his legless body along on a similar contraption, propelling himself with his hands to which he has strapped wooden blocks.

At a sharp zigzag in the Lane there is a collapsed building over to the left, seemingly untouched since the day it fell many years ago. It has since become an unofficial rubbish tip inhabited by free running chickens, cats and dogs, all living in apparent harmony.

Past this at number 36, on the right, is the 'Country Spirit Shop'; an unusual presence in a Muslim quarter. Either side of the entrance door is piled high with freshly harvested goat skins and you will need to push aside hanging carcases in order to gain access. All this seems to do the business no harm, it being well patronised by the thirsty.

A little further on Harin Bari Lane ends in a tee junction with Tiretta Bazar Lane (signed also as Street). Turning left and wandering eastwards one passes numerous open air catering enterprises interspersed with yet more open fronted butchers shops, each with a few patient dogs and cats sitting expectantly in front.

Generally, there are more beggars in evidence here than in Harin Bari Lane, possibly explained by the presence of a nearby Mosque. The variety of disabilities on display can be quite disturbing on first encounter. From amputated limbs or severe facial disfigurement to leprous stumps being waved at passers by. Quite apart from these terrible afflictions, some are also blind. There is one relatively mobile chap who has become a familiar sight to me. He shuffles along with the aid of a stout wooden stave to which he has attached a bicycle bell which he uses with great effect to draw attention to his blindness.

Just where the Lane performs a left/right chicane there is the wonderfully named barber's shop, the 'Al Aleeza Handsomes Corner'. Right next door is 'Mr Farook Chicken Centre' with his clucking stock crammed into stacked cages either side of the entrance door.

The Lane runs out as it nears the junction with Phears Lane. Turning sharp right here into Sri Nath Babu Lane, the observant will notice a few, mainly elderly people, of unmistakably Chinese appearance. This is the start of what little is left of Calcutta's old central China Town.

The Chinese came to Calcutta quite early on in the 19th century, mainly from Canton Province. Many came as leather workers and even today most of the shoe shops in Bentinck Street remain in Chinese hands. Most of the younger members of Calcutta's Chinese community have long since left this central area for Tangra out in Calcutta's eastern suburbs or moved abroad. The dwindling number remaining here are mainly the elderly.

One other small legacy of the Chinese is the presence of a number of laundries in the immediate vicinity. There is the 'Super Landry' on the right hand side of the Lane and a little further along the 'New Boxey Laundry' (high class art dyers and dry cleaners).

A right turn immediately past the 'New Boxey' brings you into Blackburn Lane. This ancient and once continuous thoroughfare was fragmented with the laying out of India Exchange Place extension and New CIT Road and the three short stretches of what remains are to be found at various locations in the vicinity. As you turn into the Lane and depending upon the time of the day, the traveller may well be confronted with a sizeable herd of goats. Although usually tethered, they often completely block the Lane and take some persuading to let you through.

In this section of Blackburn Lane there is a good deal of evidence of the Lane's historic links to Calcutta's Chinese community. Indeed, there are some still living here; their homes easily identifiable by the red painted entrance doors. At number 16, just above the red steel street door is a stone plaque identifying the building as the Chon Nee Thang Alms-house. Next door is a community centre, this time the whole building being painted bright red. Immediately past this, through a set of iron grills, can be seen the business sign of the 'Kareshma Ladies Beauty Salon', proprietor Mrs Wang Meilan. Two doors further along is another unmistakably Chinese building with bold Chinese characters carved in the lintel above the (red) doorway.

Most of the right hand side of the Lane is taken up with a remarkable old building, the upper storey of which forms an ornate arcaded balcony finished off with fine cast iron railings. The western end of this building, carrying the address of number 17, houses 'The Hupeh Association', a welfare group serving the Chinese community. The building is also home to the 'Sea Voi Yune Leong Church', the entrance to which is located just around the corner.

The Lane turns ninety degrees to the left into the last short stretch before joining the main thoroughfare of India Exchange Place extension. Before leaving the Lane, look over to the left and locate the square stone plaque set in the wall of number 14 identifying the site of the 'Chooney Thong Club'; a reminder of when the local Chinese community was more numerous.

The Lane emerges into India Exchange Place extension which just a little further east becomes New CIT Road. It was the laying out of this thoroughfare in the early 1960's by the Calcutta Improvement Trust (CIT), which fragmented many of the ancient lanes in this vicinity and decimated what was the City's original China town.

Almost opposite from where Blackburn Lane emerges into this busy thoroughfare, are two hideous multi storey buildings. One is the CIT Building, the other the BSNL Telephone Exchange: both hugely overbearing in relation to surrounding buildings. Squashed between and set slightly back from these two monstrosities, survives the premises of the 'See Ip

Association and Temple'. A community centre occupies the ground floor with the Temple taking up the upper floor. Visitors are welcome; simply walk up.

Crossing straight over India Exchange Place extension and just to the right, is another of the remaining fragments of Blackburn Lane, leading south. This is immediately recognisable by the scavenging operations going on at its entrance. Just to the left of where the Lane starts, is a small depot where the Municipal Corporation dumps trash collected locally, pending transfer to Calcutta's main dumping grounds at Dhapa out in the eastern suburbs. This depot will be swarming with ragpickers and other scavengers. Their operations spill over into the roadway. It is instructive and humbling to see just what has value to those engaged in this line of work and the pains taken to extract and sort those elements.

Over to the right of the Lane's entrance is number 20; a still handsome but once very grand building housing the 'Toong On Church' on the upper floor. Until its closure in the 1970's, the ground floor of this building housed the once famous (and some say notorious) 'Nanking Restaurant' which in the second quarter of the 20th century was apparently the place to be seen amongst Calcutta's cognoscenti.

Progressing down this fragment of Blackburn Lane towards the junction with Sun Yat Sen Street, there are increasing numbers of crudely constructed pavement shacks. Here and in the adjacent stretches of New CIT Road, (either side of the two multi storey buildings mentioned earlier), and all along the eastern arm of Sun Yat Sen Street are arguably, some of the very worst pavement bustees (slums) to be seen anywhere in Calcutta. Made up of bits of old corrugated iron, hardboard, plastic tarpaulin, rotten timber, broken brick and anything else which can be scavenged, these appalling shacks lack even the most basic of amenities for civilised existence and yet house whole extended families. All use open fires for cooking and, being jammed so tightly together, are a fire tragedy waiting to happen, more so given the highly flammable nature of their construction materials.

Just before reaching the junction with Sun Yat Sen Street and over to the right, there is a lady who makes a living by straightening out reclaimed nails. She sits there on the pavement with her small iron block and hammer and a pile of bent and rusty nails (possibly a by product of the recycling witnessed in Ismail Madan Lane in chapter 3). Straightening the nails with remarkable skill she sells these on by weight. I have been on nodding terms with her for about ten years and, on recent visits, have noticed she has been joined by one of her daughters in the enterprise.

At the junction with Sun Yat Sen Street there is a long line of more terrible pavement bustees stretching away eastwards. Periodically these will be cleared away by the authorities but will gradually be rebuilt by the inhabitants. Where else are they to go? Just to the right of the junction, on the opposite side of the Street are a number of tiny shops serving the surviving Chinese community, some of whose members will be taking tea here. The oldest established of these shops is the 'Hap Hing Co. Chinese provisions and medicines store.'

Crossing straight over the junction, the traveller will enter the first arm of the legendary Chaatawalla Gullee. So notorious was the past reputation of the Gullee that it was said that in bygone days, parents exasperated at the behaviour of their children, would threaten banishment to the Gullee; in imagination 'the lowest pit of hell to which everything wicked was relegated.'

Passing down the Gullee, there are a number of unwholesome butchers' shops followed by half a dozen or so tiny retail outlets. Taking the turning on the right leads into a far narrower section of the Gullee, mainly residential. The tiny dwellings here house such numbers of people as would seem impossible; one of the reasons why so much daytime life here takes place outside. There are also some interesting small enterprises here. 'Plastics Paradise' is one; 'heaven in all things plastic.' There is a tiny noodle factory and a number of timber and copper wire reclamation concerns.

By the time the public water pump is reached, the Gullee will be filled with scores of children playing and groups of women laundering clothes, cooking or just gossiping. It is a lively place which I always enjoy passing through having now become to be on friendly terms with a number of the families. A few trips back I was accorded the huge honour of being invited to attend the wedding of the daughter of one such family. A lively affair it was as well.

A little further onwards the Gullee narrows even more until it becomes little more than a passageway, then suddenly gives out onto Rabindra Sarani, close to the Lalbazar/BB Ganguly Street crossing.

To return to the starting point, simply turn right and when the now familiar Nakhoda Mosque comes into sight, you will be close to the Colotolla Street junction from where you began.

Chapter 5

COLOTOLLA STREET TO GIRI BABU LANE

The best starting point is the same used in the previous chapter; the junction of Colotolla Street with Rabindra Sarani.

For the traveller who has not already made this discovery, this location is perfect for photographing Calcutta street life. You have the milling crowds pouring in and out of Colotolla Street and Armenian Street almost opposite, merging with the crowds flowing each way along Rabindra Sarani. There will be carts, rickshaws, trucks and taxis together with the odd tram, grinding and clanking southwards down Rabindra Sarani with the looming Nakhoda Mosque as backdrop. This procession will be meeting a similar vehicular scrum moving northwards towards MG Road and beyond. Weaving between all this will be coolies, either singly or in groups, manually transporting loads which almost anywhere else on earth would be considered impossible. I could stand watching this all day and never tire of this kaleidoscope of street life.

Walking eastwards from the starting point along Colotolla Street, seek out the fourth turning on the right, which is Phears

Lane. This is immediately past Kalutola Lane and almost exactly the point where Colotolla Street becomes Maulana Saukat Ali Lane.

Phears Lane is an ancient thoroughfare which, apart from traffic, seems hardly unchanged since it was laid out a couple of centuries back. The Lane can become madly congested at certain times of the day and, as with so many similar locations in Calcutta, there is always something interesting to seek out there. One such place can be found at number 63, directly opposite the 'Kol Guest House'. This is the premises of a bidi maker. Bidis are the cigarette of the poor, a few strands of rough tobacco wrapped in a leaf then tied with cotton into bundles of five or ten. This is a good place to witness the manufacturing process. The bidi maker works with great speed and formidable dexterity; very difficult given the flimsiness of the component parts. Having tried to do it and making a rare mess of it, I can speak with experience on just how fiddly the operation is. Nimble fingers are required and for this reason many young children are engaged in the trade. The observant traveller will see evidence of this throughout the City's backstreet workshops dedicated to this trade.

Around about this part of the Lane it is instructive to spend a few minutes having a look at the tangles of external electrical wiring festooning the frontages of some of the buildings just above head height. How it would be possible to trace any fault in these confusing jumbles just beggars belief. That aside, the risk from fire or electrocution must be considerable. This is not far fetched for whilst in Calcutta on this latest visit, a lady pedestrian was killed in a nearby street after stepping on an exposed live cable in the roadway.

Reaching the first turning on the left off the Lane, (Kabi Raj Row) it is worth having a look down the turning at the green painted and highly ornate canopied balcony set at first floor level on one of the buildings. There are many such architectural gems to be found hereabouts many, like this one, now sadly decayed.

Close by the next turning on the left (Debendra Mullick Lane), is the premises of the 'Naim Tea Stall'. Here you can purchase a small 'bhand' (the small, shallow earthenware single use cup to be seen by their thousands littering the City's gutters) for four rupees. A large 'bhand' will set you back six rupees and, for the proprietor's cosmopolitan customers, an ordinary cupful can be had for five rupees. Mr Naim must have had trouble with debtors in the past, judging by his prominent sign warning, in large capital letters 'NO CREDIT'.

All along the Lane, it is worth looking upwards now and again to take in some of the once fine upper storey balconies, many boasting ornate cast iron railings. As with so much in the older quarters of Calcutta, you have to look beyond the decay and dereliction to appreciate the value of much of what exists.

As Phears Lane nears the junction with New CIT Road, a look over to the left reveals a collection of truly terrible pavement bustees. These continue out into New CIT Road itself, both to the left and right. To my certain knowledge these have existed here for at least the last ten years and still there is no evidence of even the most basic amenities having been provided for those unfortunate enough to have to occupy these hovels.

Just before crossing over the junction, look to the right to locate 'Abdulla Remedies', a kind of pharmacy offering remedies for an eclectic mix of maladies from sexual dysfunction to baldness and acne. Mr Abdullah has helpfully listed the full range on a neat display board placed prominently outside the premises.

Crossing the New CIT Road junction, Phears Lane continues southwards, beginning a gently curve to the right then crossing the eastern end of Sun Yat Sen Street. Once across this latter junction, the curve in the Lane becomes more pronounced, passing the Ling Liang Chinese High School and Church of the same name and, to the right, a modern multi storey white building, almost cylindrical in shape and wholly incongruous with surrounding buildings. The remaining short section of the Lane is taken up with pavement workshops engaged in the repair of those manual, pedal tricycle carts used for transporting goods and intrinsic to the street scene in much of the City.

As the curve of the Lane ends, so does the Lane itself, merging into Hide Lane after a ninety degree turn to the left. The short stretch of Hide Lane contains a number of dealers in what can best be described as architectural salvage. There are doors, windows, other timber fittings, ironwork grills and so on, stacked all over the left hand side of the Lane. Amongst all this can often be found some very fine items; intricately carved wooden door frames, ornate cast iron panels, screening and the like. Over to the left is a peculiar small structure signed as 'Police Beat House' which I am given to understand was a kind of ancient lock up.

Hide Lane soon spills out into BB Ganguly Street (still known to many by its old name of Bow Bazar Street). Turning left and heading eastwards along BB Ganguly Street to the third turning on the left, which is Giri Babu Lane. The narrow turning into the Lane is just before the major junction with CR Avenue which will be seen immediately ahead.

Giri Babu Lane is a narrow, winding backwater, in parts little more than a passageway. It is usually teeming with people, both local residents and the visiting faithful summoned to prayer at the tall narrow Mosque improbably squeezed in further along the Lane.

My friend Udita once accompanied me on a walk all along the Lane. There would be times when I would catch her giving me a quizzical look whenever she could not for the life of her see why something interested me; this was one of those times.

Along the Lane is an interesting repair works for hand pulled rickshaws, easy to locate by the component parts of these iconic machines piled in heaps outside. If the workshop is open, just walk in and have a look at what is going on; no one seems to mind such intrusion.

The western traveller negotiating Giri Babu Lane is a rare sight for the inhabitants and will attract a lot of good natured attention, particularly from the large groups of children always present. There really is no danger of getting lost despite the bewildering twists and turns and blind offshoots. The only place the Lane can emerge is onto CR Avenue; just follow the flow of those passing through.

Giri Babu Lane finally ends where it emerges out into CR Avenue about fifty metres south of the main junction with Sun Yat Sen Street and New CIT Road to the left and Eden Hospital Road to the right on the opposite side of the Avenue. There is a rather grand statue at the junction, set behind iron railings on a kind of island in the roadway. The Statue is of Maharana Pratap Singh, a Hindu Rajput ruler of what is present day Rajasthan.

Immediately past the statue, on either side of CR Avenue are the two northern entrances to Central Metro Station. This is also a good spot from which to locate a taxi.

Chapter 6

MECHUA BAZAR

The starting point here is the now familiar major junction of CR Avenue and MG Road; in this case the north eastern corner of the junction.

Heading northwards along CR Avenue, the first turning to the right is Sambhu Chatterji Street. This is immediately recognisable on two visual counts.

Firstly, at the entrance to the Street will be huge piles of neatly stacked timber; the product of dismantled packing cases, pallets and other wooden containers. This could quite easily be the product of all the industry witnessed in Ismail Madan Lane described earlier in chapter 3. Here however these materials are in their second stage of recycling, being fashioned into new boxes and other containers for some alternative use.

The second visual clue is the presence of rather a lot of used mustard oil tins; tens of thousands of them in fact, stacked in huge piles three and four metres high. As all this is being taken in, there will be chaps arriving with even more of the tins, some on foot carrying a kind of yoke contraption from which hang dozens of tins all roped together. Others will be arriving on those pedal tricycle carts which will be loaded with tottering piles of tins, swaying alarmingly as they manoeuvre their transport through the throng.

Progressing eastwards along the Street, there begins the initial process in recycling these oil tins. This involves washing out the oil residues. There will be dozens of people squatting whilst scrubbing the containers with soapy and invariably filthy water. A little further on there will be another branch of the trade wielding hammers and similar implements, flattening out those oil tins considered beyond reasonable repair. These will end up in some local smelting facility for their metal content.

The Street and all its offshoots form the poor and predominantly Muslim quarter of Mechua Bazar. The indicators of poverty are striking even by inner city Calcutta standards. The buildings lining either side of the Street are overcrowded, crudely constructed, decayed and crumbling; it is a wonder some are still standing. It is hardly surprising that most activity seems to take place out in the street itself. Cooking fires, steaming cauldrons, great pans of spluttering cooking oil are everywhere. Between all this are pavement barbers shaving lathered clients, scavenging rag pickers, wandering goats, chickens and dogs and the inevitable throngs of small children. There are tiny, street level workshops engaged in all sorts of trades; printing, leatherwork metal bashing and grinding and, oddly, some undefined processes involving large quantities of sheet cardboard.

Ahead, and blocking further forward progress looms the rear of the, as yet unfinished, College Street Mall. This occupies the space which was once the bustling College Street market, long since swept away.

When further advance becomes impossible, it is necessary to turn to the left into the remaining short section of Sambhu Chatterji Street. This soon meets Madan Mohan Burman Street, the main east west artery hereabouts between CR Avenue and Bidhan Sarani.

Almost but not quite opposite, is the entrance to Balak Dutta Lane Bustee (and signed as such). The entrance to the Lane itself opens up just to the left of this sign. The Bustee itself is a frightful place but of considerable interest and certainly warrants a look. Hugely overcrowded, it is difficult to determine any demarcation between street life and domestic privacy; leaving the distinct impression that you are wandering about people's private living quarters. Even so, no one seems to mind your presence in the least.

Back in Balak Dutta Lane proper, this narrow teeming byway is lined either side by dozens of tiny workshops engaged in all manner of interesting small scale trades. It is very easy to get sidetracked here, trying to determine just what each of the workshops are producing or assembling and what part the efforts of those engaged there are contributing to some unexplained larger process. There is the chap who is churning out rubber straps for flip flops, nothing else, just the straps. There is another operation a little further on which is stamping out bottle tops from an antique looking metal press; yet another is varnishing paint brush handles.

Wandering further along the Lane, there can be seen, over to the right, what must once have been a very grand building. What it was used for in a locality such as this can only be guessed at. The structure is of red brick but it appears this was once covered in a stucco, perhaps to imitate stonework. At roof level are four large stone Grecian urns above a plaque which dates the building at 1920. Five large columns are formed into the frontage, each with Corinthian capitals at first and top storey level. All this is set off with a heavy fancy cornice running along the frontage at eaves level.

Next door is another similarly incongruous although wholly different building. Of vaguely art deco design, this building rises through four levels with a bold square bay rising from ground to roof level. Set in this bay is a narrow and decorative metal framed window stretching unbroken the entire height of the building. This feature is very reminiscent of that to be found on many a fine Odeon Cinema building, once to be found all over London and the home counties.

Reaching the end of the Lane, a left turn takes you into the eastern end of Muktaram Babu Street; a wider more open thoroughfare than what has gone before. Passing the entrance to Muktaram Babu Lane to the left, seek out the next turning on the left which is Mitra Lane. It will now be evident that the route followed, if viewed from above, has been rectangular.

Mitra Lane is home to the skilled end of the mustard oil tin recycling industry, the initial stages of which were witnessed at the start of this walk. All along the right hand side of the Lane are enormous piles of the refurbished tins, all neatly stacked, awaiting collection and reuse.

The left hand side of the Lane is taken up with numerous workshops of highly skilled tinsmiths putting the finishing touches to the recycled product or manufacturing new ones. It is an activity well worth watching. New bottoms, or tops or handles are being carefully cut out and fashioned and dents are being removed. The tins are then passed to the chaps with their old fashioned heavy soldering irons being heated over charcoal burners. One quick continuous swipe with the iron and a new top or bottom is fixed to the body of the tin or a previously suspect seam is permanently sealed. The process is made to look easy, even casual but requires great skill, particularly given the basic nature of the tools and materials being used.

Crossing the junction with Munshi Sadaruddin Lane, Mitra Lane continues until it meets the lower end of Madan Mohan Burman Street. Cross straight over into Kalabagan Bustee New Road. This short thoroughfare is usually packed with ragpickers and other scavengers sorting through and separating their collections into various piles ready to be sold on. There is also generally a lot of livestock in the Road; goats, chickens, dogs and cats all scavenging among whatever has been discarded.

On reaching the end of the Road, turn right and you are back in Sambhu Chatterji Street close to the point from which you started.

Chapter 7

MECHUA FRUIT MARKET

A convenient starting point is the north western corner of the CR Avenue/MG Road junction; in fact directly opposite the point where the walk described in the previous chapter started and ended.

This little expedition is best undertaken in the first part of the morning when the Market is in full swing. From about 11 am onwards the Market starts to wind down. Many will find this walk quite arduous and for this reason it has been kept as short as possible without losing any of the atmosphere involved.

The Mechua wholesale fruit market sprawls through the pullulating lanes which lay between CR Avenue and Rabindra Sarani and behind the northern frontage of MG Road.

The Market is the largest of its kind in the State, daily shifting enormous tonnages of pineapples, pomegranates, melons, papaya and jackfruit and whatever else happens to be in season. When the various types of mango begin to arrive, upwards of 800 tons of this fruit alone will be traded here daily.

The entire length and breadth of the Market is a maelstrom of activity. Once caught up in it all, you are swept along with the armies of coolies transporting (usually on their heads), huge boxes or baskets of various fruits. They are in a hurry and it does not do to get in their way. This coupled with the press of buyers, sellers or simply onlookers like yourself make it not the sort of place for the claustrophobic who finds crowded spaces intimidating. Even so, the Market being contained on three sides by major thoroughfares means there are plenty of escape routes to relative tranquillity if it all becomes too much.

From the starting point walk northwards along CR Avenue, taking the first turning on the left into Syed Sally Lane. It should be noted that, confusingly, there are several other seemingly different thoroughfares in the immediate vicinity also bearing this name.

Immediately upon entering the Lane you are engulfed in the Market's hustle and bustle. There will be streams of goods going in both directions, in and out of the Market; carried manually or piled on bicycles, carts, barrows, rickshaws and motor vehicles. Negotiating your way through all this is made all the more difficult by badly parked lorries, many in the process of being loaded or unloaded.

Keeping over to the left (if you can), follow the line of buildings left then immediately left into Balmukund Makkar Road. Here you will find a lot of dealers in dates; great huge sticky masses of dates everywhere the eye is cast; often covered in swarms of flies. Next to these sticky messes are placed smouldering ends of bits of old rope, designed to deter flies and proving hopelessly ineffective.

You will find here as in most other of the Market's thoroughfares, the road surfaces are strewn with straw. A good idea to help soak up the rotten and trodden in fruit underfoot but with a downside that it conceals potholes and other irregularities; so proceed with caution.

MECHUA FRUIT MARKET

When you can see the end of the Road, where it spills out into Rabindra Sarani, look over to the right for the turning into Chitpur Spur. Along the Spur can be found the 'Ritu Raj Hotel' which claims 'Pleasure of a Homely Stay'. One could be forgiven for having doubts on this extravagant declaration given the Hotel's horrendously noisy location, uninviting outward appearance and general environment.

Just past the Hotel, turn right into Madan Mohan Burman Street. This is the main thoroughfare through the Market which will be rejoined after circuiting the next block. Over to the left is the entrance to Ballar Das Street. This is often jam packed with lorries and carts, replenishing supplies to the stalls in the vicinity. There is much evidence here of imported fruit; apples from China, other fruits from Bangladesh, Malaysia and beyond.

At the end of the Street, turn right into Munshi Sadaruddin Street and at the next crossroads, sharp right into Balmukund Makkar Road (which presumably was once linked to the stretch of road of the same name encountered earlier). If you are early enough, this part of the Market will be crowded with auctioneers and buyers engaged in the secret signals of transaction known only to them. The auctioneers, often sat high up on the backs of lorries will be scanning the crowd before them for subtle signs from potential buyers. Keep your hands firmly in your pockets lest you unwittingly find you are the reluctant owner of half a ton of jackfruit. At the back edge of the crowd will be the waiting coolies, heads piled high with boxes or baskets of whatever is being auctioned. At a signal from the successful bidder, they will tear off to load the buyer's vehicle then rush back for their next commission.

Making your way down the Road, you will pass mountains of pineapples, bananas and boxed fruit piled anything up to 4 or 5 metres high; the scale is truly staggering.

Where the Road rejoins Madan Mohan Burman Street, turn sharp left, walking east in the direction of CR Avenue. A great deal of pavement side catering takes place along here. Huge cauldrons of rice being stirred with what looks like a dinghy oar; gigantic wok like vessels filled with bubbling and smoking oil all afloat with swelling puris. This is also the spot where, if you are lucky, you will witness a performance from itinerant street entertainers. This often takes the form of a tightrope being strung up, on which the invariably young, 'artistes' then perform amazing balancing acts.

Just before the Road ends at CR Avenue there will be a number of pavement barbers, cutting hair and shaving faces with old fashioned cut throat razors. Some operate from upturned crates; others, more established in the trade, provide a proper chair for their clients. Should the traveller wish to avail themselves of such a service here or at the many other street locations throughout the City, it is advisable to carry your own razor rather than rely on that in general use by the barber.

Once back in CR Avenue, your starting point lies about one hundred metres to the right, past an ornate Mosque and a commanding water tank, raised high above the Avenue off the back edge of the pavement.

Chapter 8

ARMENIAN STREET TO THE WRITERS' BUILDING

A convenient starting point for this exploration is the south western corner of the junction of MG Road with Rabindra Sarani.

To complete the whole of this route should take about two hours, a little longer than many of those walks described in other chapters of this book. Depending upon time available to you, it is quite possible to split the walk into two stages. The first stage would take you from the starting point to the Armenian Church and the second from the Church to Dalhousie Square and the Writers Building.

Head off southwards down Rabindra Sarani in the direction of the landmark Nakhoda Mosque, clearly visible in the distance. The first main turning to the left is Tarachand Dutta Street. Cross straight over Rabindra Sarani at this point and the entrance to Armenian Street is dead ahead.

This ancient narrow Street runs all the way from here to the Armenian Church, located just beyond Brabourne Road. Armenian Street is generally regarded as one of the most madly congested in the whole of Calcutta and is full of atmosphere. Here there are large numbers of pedestrians, with or without unwieldy loads; overloaded barrows and carts being pushed, pulled or otherwise manhandled, often by a team of several coolies; bicycles and rickshaws and the whole panoply of motorised transport. Weaving amongst all this will be itinerant hawkers, the odd cow or goat and gangs of street dogs.

It is not at all unusual for the Street to become jammed solid, resulting in nothing, not even unencumbered pedestrians being able to move. I have witnessed this many times in many visits; perhaps you will be as lucky for it really is an experience. When this occurs, to add to the mayhem every vehicle will start sounding their horns; others ringing bicycle and rickshaw bells and generally voicing impatience. Just when you begin to think it is all hopeless and almost as if some giant plug had been pulled, the whole crazy jumble suddenly frees itself and begins to move.

Right at the start of the Street there are a number of tobacco merchants and dealers in Tendu leaves; a major component in the manufacture of bidis, the cigarette of the poor in India.

Just past these tobacco dealers' premises and over to the right is the Sagar Guest House, set back from the Street down a grimy and uninviting cul de sac. If you are dissatisfied with your current Calcutta accommodation, call into the Guest House and ask to see a room; in all likelihood this will dispel any misgivings you may have been harbouring.

Once past the junction with R C Roy Street over to the right, Armenian Street starts noticeably to narrow. Over to the left is the ornate, cream and green painted Armenian Street Mosque. To get a half reasonable view of the fine dome and minarets will involve you squeezing hard over against the buildings opposite, given the narrowness of the thoroughfare.

Just past the Mosque, on the right hand side of the Street there is a magnificently and ornately carved gateway leading into a cul de sac of godowns. This gateway is surmounted by very pleasing oval bays at third and fourth floor levels, complete with mock Corinthian style columns to either side. The whole effect is only a little spoiled by the veritable jungle of external electrical wiring hanging in tangled hanks all along the top of the gateway.

At the next junction, look to your right down Mullick Street, and note the huge old mansion building, its frontage adorned with eight proud columns; almost the last thing you would expect to find hereabouts. This of course is part of the magic of Calcutta; its ability constantly to surprise you.

Past this junction you quickly meet the turning on your left into Portuguese Street. This is worth a short diversion to get a view of the magnificent Cathedral Church of Our Lady of the Rosary; more commonly known as the Portuguese Church. Built in the closing years of the 18th century, the Church replaced and even earlier chapel on this site.

Back in Armenian Street, look over to your left at the nearby corner property and the highly ornate first floor balcony which sweeps around the entire frontage of the building, supported from below by a series of ornately carved corbels. Next door at number 11A is another once fine building with a pretty gateway. Unfortunately the whole effect is spoiled by the jumble of exposed wiring festooning the frontage.

Just a short distance on, the Street meets Brabourne Road which must be crossed to access the remaining portion of Armenian Street. Brabourne Road has been officially renamed Biplabi Trailakya Maharaj Sarani, altogether too much of a mouthful and, anyway, virtually unknown as such to locals. We will stick with Brabourne Road.

Most street maps, even online versions will show the continuation of Armenian Street, our onward route, as being directly opposite the section from which you have just emerged. This is not the case. You will need to walk to the right along Brabourne Road, keeping a look out for the white tower of the

Armenian Church rising above the buildings on the opposite side of the Road. When you spot it, position yourself directly opposite, and cross straight over the Road to find the elusive remaining section of Armenian Street.

This short remaining stretch of Armenian Street is by far the narrowest so far encountered and is packed tightly with the premises of small traders. One of the two entrances into the Church can be found here but it is discreetly placed opposite number 48. There is a small stone plaque just to the right of the entrance gateway dating the Church to 1707. It is not clear if this date is intended to relate to the existing Church or the original wooden structure which predated the existing building by at least a couple of decades. Even so, this makes the Armenian Church one of the oldest in the City.

Once you have signed the visitors' book, you pass through the entrance archway out into the surprisingly spacious churchyard. This is paved entirely with the gravestones of members of Calcutta's Armenian community, some dating back to the early 18th century. One gravestone is even older and can be found just to the right of the entrance to the Church itself. This marks the tomb of Reza Bibi 'wife of the late charitable Sookias' and is dated 1630. If this is accurate, and there are many authorities who dispute this, then this would have put the Armenians in Calcutta many decades before Job Charnock dropped anchor and planted the British Flag on the east Bank of the Hooghly at Sutanuti.

If you are particularly lucky during your visit you will encounter the knowledgeable Church caretaker. He is a mine of information both as regards the history of the Church and that of Calcutta's remaining but dwindling Armenian community, which currently numbers around two hundred.

On leaving through the Churchyard gateway back into Armenian Street, head left towards where the Street meets Pandit Parashottam Roy Street, which quickly morphs into

Old China Bazar Street. Looking back at this point gives a fine view of the Church Tower, rising serenely above all the chaos which surrounds it.

Continue southwards down Old China Bazar Street, passing the scores of premises trading in all manner of stationery; calendars, diaries and every type of writing materials. When you reach number 141, look opposite to locate the tiny narrow entrance into Synagogue Street. This ancient little thoroughfare is well worth the short diversion involved. It no longer houses a Synagogue; the City's two remaining being the Beth El (1856) in Pollack Street and Magen David (1884) in Canning Street, both quite nearby. Calcutta's long standing Jewish community once numbered more than six thousand. This has now shrunk to no more than thirty souls and is dwindling with each passing year. Walk right down to end of Synagogue Street to obtain an excellent view across Brabourne Road, to the frontage of the Portuguese Church, visited earlier.

Retracing your steps back along Synagogue Street, turn left back into Old China Bazar Street keeping an eye on the shop names and their often eclectic stock in trade. 'Novelty Store' at number 141 deals in, amongst other things, diaries, toy guns, fireworks, flags and election materials. 'Tulsidas Paul Grandsons' at number 159 are dealers in both umbrellas and fireworks whilst electrical goods may be had at the premises of Obhoy Churn Coondo at number 207. Perhaps my favourite is at number 214 where Rajabally Lookmanjee and Co. trade in glassware.

The Street crosses the junction with Canning Street where can be found numerous traders in Peacock feathers. This must be about as legally questionable as hawking lumps of coral but it is all conducted quite openly and seems to be tolerated.

Just past the junction with Canning Street, and above the frontages of numbers 188 to 191 is what must have been the very grand trading premises of 'Nandalal Paul Bros. – General

Merchants, established 1890'. They had a solid confidence in their world back then. Their buildings were a statement of that and an indication that they intended to be around for a long time. I admire that and am rather sorry at its passing.

Further along the Street, the predominant trade turns to glass and mirrors. There are gangs of men manoeuvring huge panes of glass from lorries into premises in the Street and adjoining side lanes. Often you cannot see the glass and it all looks like one of those games played as a child (well at least I did), carrying those imaginary panes of glass past confused passers by. Like so much else in Calcutta all this glass transporting is done entirely manually yet I have never seen a breakage occur.

At its end, the Street emerges into the very busy India Exchange Place. Turn right here then left into Netaji Subhas Road, effectively walking anti clockwise around the block. At the next junction, turn left into the northern side of Dalhousie Square (BBD Bagh), with the iconic Writers' Building to your left.

The Writers' Building is so called as the original purpose of the building was to house the clerks or 'writers' of the East India Company. The building now houses the Secretariat of the West Bengal State Government. Completed in 1880 to a design by a certain Colonel St.Clair Wilkins it replaced an earlier white plastered structure. Before that, the Company's writers were accommodated within the old Fort William which stood to the west between this spot and the Hooghly.

Immediately past the Writers' Building is the glistening white, landmark, St Andrew's Church, standing right on the busy junction of Brabourne Road and Lalbazar Street. This is the finishing point and also the starting point for the expedition described in the next chapter.

Chapter 9

IN AND AROUND DALHOUSIE SQUARE

Little opportunity is provided here for making use of backstreet routes; few now exist in what is the very heart of the City's oldest and most historically significant quarter.

Taking in most of what in the early 18th century, was known as 'White Town' or the European quarter, this walk involves a clockwise circuit of BBD Bagh or Dalhousie Square to use its former name and that still in most common usage. Added to this is an area to the south and west of the Square which includes the historic St John's Church.

The Square which has formed the central feature of the town plan of Calcutta since the City's inception, was originally known as 'Tank Square' and before that, 'The Park'. It was later renamed after Lord Dalhousie, the Governor General of India from 1848 to 1856. It was officially renamed BBD Bagh in honour of three young nationalist martyrs, Benoy, Badal and Dinesh who in 1930, shot dead the Inspector General of Prisons at the Writers' Building on the northern side of the Square.

The starting point is St Andrew's Church (where the last walk ended), located on the north east corner of the Square, adjacent to the Writers' Building and hard by the junction of Brabourne Road, Lalbazar Street and the Square itself.

The elegant Church with its lofty spire, often referred to as the 'Scottish Church' is one of the landmark buildings of the area. The Church is built on the site once occupied by an early 18th century court building, recognised in the naming of the thoroughfare leading south as 'Old Court House Street' (now renamed Hermanta Bose Sarani – arguably meaningless to any other then the renamers themselves).

From the Church entrance cross over the road to the Square itself. Immediately to the right and thankfully largely hidden from view, is a relatively newly constructed parking lot; hardly a fitting use for a site of such high conservation value. Ahead and forming the eastern side of the Square, is a large central bus station which, surprisingly fits in well in this setting. To the right, west of the bus station and set centrally within the Square, is Lal Dighi or the 'great tank' as it was originally known to the British. It is not actually a Dighi (lake) but a rather large pond fed by a natural spring. Centuries ago it provided fish for the Governor's House set within the walls of the old Fort William, located just to the west between the Square and the river. It is said that the 'tank' was excavated in 1709 and that its waters were reputedly the sweetest in the then emerging City.

The Municipal Corporation has recently completed a makeover of Lal Dighi. This involved dredging the 'tank', installing seven fountains in the centre and creating a fine promenade along the western bank. Sets of benches have been provided along the banks making this a pleasant oasis in the heart of the City.

As you come level with the southern side of the Square, you see over to the right, the truly hideous Telephone Bhaven; a building of unremitting ugliness, completely out of keeping with the architecture of the Square and wrecking the view north to the Writers' Building and St Andrew's Church.

Continuing on and over to the left is the fine colonnaded frontage of the famous Great Eastern Hotel (now called the Lalit Great Eastern). This fine heritage, landmark hotel had been closed for several years whilst undergoing complete refurbishment. Although reopened towards the end of 2013, work on the oldest part of the building will continue for a further two years and as I write, the lower levels of the fine old frontage facing you, are concealed by shuttering. The Hotel's new main lobby can now be found in a new block accessed off Abdul Hamed Street just around the corner.

The history of the Great Eastern Hotel, India's oldest, is inextricably linked to that of the City. First opened in 1840 by an Englishman, David Wilson, it was initially named the Auckland Hotel after the Governor General of the day. Despite this, it was always popularly known as 'Wilson's Hotel' until, in 1860, it was renamed the Great Eastern. In 1883 it became the first hotel in India to be illuminated by electricity. The Great Eastern became a byword for taste, elegance and luxury; a favourite haunt of Calcutta's elite.

The Hotel began its slow decline from the 1960's. By the 1970's it was facing financial ruin and had to be rescued, first by being taken over by the State Government before being finally nationalised in 1980.

As luck would have it, my wife and I were fortunate enough to last stay at the Great Eastern in the final year of the hotel's operation before it closed for refurbishment. Then this labyrinthine old warren of a place was certainly dated and decaying; rather like a once beautiful old Dowager but was still magnificent. I greatly miss the old place but warmly applaud what has been achieved by the Lalit Group in preserving what could and should be preserved and ensuring the continuation of this wonderful old institution into the 21st century and beyond.

Almost opposite the old entrance to the Great Eastern and to the right, is Larkin Lane. This location used to be the pitch of a lady beggar who I became so accustomed to seeing that she had almost become part of the street scene. She was blind, perhaps in her fifties and always respectably groomed and clothed. I used to wonder who assisted in getting her to her spot every morning and then returned to take her home at the end of her day. She had been there for years then, on one of my visits, she had vanished and has not since reappeared.

As you walk westwards down Larkin Lane, this becomes Pannalal Banerji Lane (formerly known, for some long forgotten reason, as Fancy Lane). Leading off of this Lane was once a thoroughfare with the intriguing name of Corkscrew Lane. This led through to the southern side of Dalhousie Square but not a single trace of it now remains.

Pannalal Banerji Lane ends where it joins Council House Street. Directly opposite this junction is St John's Church or the 'Stone Church' as it is popularly known. To access the Church, cross Council House Street and, turning left, walk to the next junction (K S Roy Street) where the Churchyard gates are to be found. As you approach these gates, notice the noble iron railings to the right, running along the Churchyard boundary and wonder why they needed painting so garishly in blue and white.

There is a small admission charge to the Churchyard, currently ten rupees per head. The grounds are beautifully kept with mature trees, flowering shrubs and lawns. From the gateway there is a particularly fine view of the Church itself, the steeple rising above the tree line in the near distance.

The Church was built in the 1780's and ranks amongst the City's oldest. It was supposedly built to a plan adapted from London's St Martin's in the Fields Church but with modifications designed to minimise the load on the soft ground supporting the foundations. The Church and grounds provide a pleasingly tranquil setting amongst the general hubbub of the surrounding streets.

The Church occupies the site of an ancient British hospital and burial ground dating back to the 1690's. Quite apart from considerations of hygiene in such unwholesome climatic conditions, imagine the situation; being bedridden with some ghastly and quite likely fatal fever in this primitive hospital. Your only view would be that of a line of tombstones and your physical proximity to the already dead could have done little for your morale.

Inside the Church and immediately to the right is an original wooden staircase of almost spiral design leading to an internal balcony. A few years ago this was crumbling with decay but has now been beautifully restored.

Towards the altar and over to the left is the recently restored 1787 painting by the German born neo classical painter Johann Zoffani, 'The Last Supper'. Before restoration you could hardly make out any of the figures on the darkened canvas. The difference resulting from restoration is quite remarkable. Zoffani whose work can be seen in London's National and Tate Galleries, actually painted a second 'Last Supper'. This hangs in St Ann's Church in Brentford, England.

To the right of the altar are a set of fine original pews facing the recently restored organ. Spot the one reserved for Governor General Warren Hastings; not difficult given its elevated position over those intended for use by lesser mortals.

On your way out of the Church, if you can locate one of the Church officials, ask if you can have a look in the 'Hastings Room'. This room is located just to the left of the entranceway. Said to have been used by Hastings for meetings. Complete with its large original committee table and chairs, historic prints and engravings, it remains largely unchanged since Hastings' day.

Outside the Church, to the right, is an ornate marble monument to Lady Charlotte Canning, wife of the East India Company's last Governor General and the Crown's first Viceroy of India. Her actual grave is at Barrackpore, an old cantonment town some 15 kilometres or so from this spot.

In the Church grounds, just north of the Church itself, is a whitewashed and domed octagonal structure set in a neatly kept area of garden. This is Job Charnock's Mausoleum, said to be the oldest surviving piece of masonry in Calcutta.

Charnock, who died in 1692, first arrived in India in 1656. He is known to have been trading in Cossimbazar and Patna before becoming the East India Company's chief agent at Hooghly in 1685.

Whilst Job Charnock is popularly and widely celebrated as the founder of Calcutta, this claim is not without controversy, seemingly having proved inconvenient in some quarters. In 2003 this culminated in a peculiar decision in the Calcutta High Court along the lines that because 'a highly civilised society and important trading centre' had existed on the site of what was to become Calcutta prior to the arrival of Europeans, Job Charnock could not be regarded as the founder of the City. This official line appears to be widely ignored by all but a few; in my view deservedly so.

Job Charnock's daughter is also interred in the Mausoleum as is William Hamilton, a surgeon of the East India Company who died in 1717. Hamilton had cured Ferrukseer 'King of Indostan' of a 'malignant distemper'. By this act, the East India Company gained influence with the grateful King who went on to grant important rights allowing the Company to establish itself and expand its operations in Bengal.

Twenty metres or so west of the Charnock's Mausoleum is a similar but smaller, domed structure. This is the tomb of the remarkable and much married Mrs Francis Johnson or 'Begum Johnson' as she was known in her day; 'the oldest resident of Bengal, universally beloved, respected and revered'.

Born in 1725 and having first married at the tender age of 13, this remarkable lady survived four husbands. She lived on until 1812 attaining, for then, the very great age of 87 years. It is said that her whist parties were one of the sought after social engagements in the Calcutta of her day.

Back towards the Church itself and hard over to the right, close up to the boundary wall fronting Church Street, is another notable monument in the form of an obelisk. This monument is to the memory of the 123 victims and 23 survivors of the 'Black Hole of Calcutta'. The 'Black Hole' was actually a prison cell in the old Fort William. There on the night of 21st June, 1756, following the fall of Calcutta to the forces of the Nawab of Bengal, the European survivors were incarcerated. There has always been controversy as to the actual number who were crammed into the 'Black Hole'. Some schools of thought, mainly Indian, insist on a far lower number of between 40 and 70 souls whilst a few, less interested in historical accuracy, deny the event ever happened at all.

This is not the original memorial which was erected in 1760 by John Zephaniah Holwell (a survivor of the 'Black Hole' and subsequent Governor of Bengal). This stood opposite the east gate of the old Fort, close to the spot where the 'Black Hole' victims were buried. This original memorial was of brick construction and rapidly deteriorated. It was finally demolished in 1821 and, on the orders of Lord Curzon, replaced in 1901 by the present marble obelisk. This was originally sited at the north western corner of Dalhousie Square and moved to its present Churchyard location in 1940.

Leaving the Church grounds by the entrance gates, the High Court buildings and the Old Town Hall are located just one block south of this point with the Raj Bhavan, Lord Curzon's folly, one block south east.

Before turning right out of the Church gates into Church Street, stand for a moment at the junction, waiting for a change in the traffic signals. This is one of the many junctions in Calcutta where Tagore and other Bengali patriotic songs (those by Dwijendra Lal Roy featuring strongly) are played through speakers to those waiting on the red stop signal. This is an initiative from the State's Chief Minister, Mamata Bannerjee (as is the acres of blue and white paint on anything improved or restored). I have heard some pretty negative comments from various Calcuttans about the singing traffic signals but I disagree. Who knows there may be something in it; this initiative may well have a soothing and calming influence on road users. It is an interesting idea anyway and may catch on elsewhere.

Walking northwards along Church Street past numerous stationers serving the Court buildings just south of here, you come to the junction of Hare Street. Turning right here, you emerge back in Council House Street at the southern side of Dalhousie Square. The magnificent building on the opposite corner is the old headquarters of the Hong Kong and Shanghai (HSBC) Bank.

Turning left and walking along the western side of Dalhousie Square, the buildings to your left are dominated by the landmark, Calcutta General Post Office. This magnificent domed building, fronted by Corinthian columns, was constructed in the 1860's to a design by Sir Walter Granville.

The site of the General Post Office is of considerable archaeological interest since it occupies the site of the south eastern bastion of the old Fort William. Near the north east corner of the Post Office, there was once a black marble plaque identifying the exact location of the 'Black Hole' prison cell. This was removed many years ago during the course of structural alterations and was never replaced. In the yard of the Post Office, there were once fragments of the original arcades which lined the east wall of the old Fort but these have long since vanished; most likely demolished in the course of alterations.

Past the General Post Office is the northern side of Dalhousie Square, dominated by the now familiar Writers' Building. Walk past the Writers' Building to your starting point, St Andrew's Church.

Chapter 10

SONAGACHI

Sonagachi is known throughout India and beyond as Calcutta's principal red light area.

Meaning 'Golden Tree', Sonagachi has a long association with the world's oldest profession. Throughout the 18th and 19th centuries, it was the place where many a merchant housed his mistresses. Today it is a place where thousands of sex workers operate from brothels housed in crumbling and decaying buildings ranged along narrow, thronged and insalubrious lanes which make up the area.

It is probably true to say that there has been more coverage given to the small area that is Sonagachi than to the whole of the rest of North Calcutta put together. Some of this coverage has been informed and useful comment; a great deal more has not. Indeed, with some of the reportage the inaccuracies are such that you are left wondering if the commentator has ever actually visited the place or, if so, if this was from the back seat of a taxi.

Provided the traveller adopts a common sense approach and an etiquette grounded in basic good manners, navigating Sonagachi during daylight hours, need present no difficulties.

Do not point cameras; it will be considered impolite and not appreciated. After dark, Sonagachi takes on a different and less predictable character. It is then the area receives its biggest influx of potential clients, many of whom will have been drinking, sometimes heavily. At these times the traveller is best advised to give the area a wide berth. It is very easy to get lost in the lanes of Calcutta after dark unless you really know where you are going. This is not the place to risk that happening.

A convenient starting point for this little expedition, is the south western corner of the junction of Jatindra Mohan (JM) Avenue (which is the northern extension of the familiar CR Avenue) and Sri Aurobinda Sarani (erstwhile Grey Street). This lies just south of the Sovabazar Metro station.

Walking westwards along Sri Aurobinda Sarani, take the first turning on the left into Abinash Kaviraj Street. This Street actually leads straight into the heart of the red light area. However there is more to Sonagachi than just that and it is worth taking a more circuitous route to appreciate those other aspects.

Passing firstly the 'Modern Dry Cleaners' to your right, then a little further along, their competitors in trade, 'Shantilal Repairing House and Dry Cleaners', take the second turning on the right into Joy Mitra Street (sometimes signed on premises in its archaic form 'Joy Mitter Street').

This ancient serpentine thoroughfare gives you a good idea what this part of Calcutta must have looked like a century or more ago; so little in the built environment seems to have changed. The old, mainly residential, buildings lining each side of the Street are reminders of a bygone age. Many have upper storeys projecting out into the Street; some with highly decorative ironwork fittings. Amongst these buildings, there are some which must have been very grand in their day; again you have to look beyond their current decayed condition.

Over to the right is one such building occupying a prominent corner plot. This has a beautiful curved balcony spanning the entire frontage. The fine ironwork railings to this balcony are repeated in the huge supporting brackets beneath it. There are eleven such brackets in all with number twelve missing.

There is another, slightly less grand frontage at number 11, now so neglected that it has a range of sizeable shrubbery growing from the brickwork a parapet level.

Number 8F, to the left, has an attractive frontage with an ornate entranceway surmounted with a stone semi-circular balcony and the remains of mock columns and fancy capitals. It is in such obviously poor structural condition, riven with many wide cracks in the masonry, that it is a miracle it is still standing. It is one of those buildings that once you are familiar with it, you automatically cross to the far side pavement when passing it.

Some of the Street's buildings are set well back from the building line and accessed via narrow passageways leading off the back edge of the pavement.

After many twists and turns (I counted ten in all), Joy Mitra Street emerges into bustling Rabindra Sarani. Turning left you pass a number of enterprises involved in repairing and renovating old safes; some of which are of huge proportions. I have often wondered how they move these about, since I have never witnessed the action nor seen any evidence of heavy lifting equipment. Most of these safes must weigh tons.

Take the next turning on the left into Masjid Bari Street. This runs roughly parallel with Joy Mitra Street and has almost as many twists and turns. There the similarity ends; there is nothing which has ever been remotely grand here. This (western) end of the Street is a grubby narrow thoroughfare, crammed with tiny workshops emitting various tapping, grinding and banging sounds and reeking of various strong solvents; a glue sniffer's paradise.

As you progress along the Street, keep an eye to the right where you pass the entrances to three narrow, squalid and dank lanes, lined with festering decayed buildings. These by lanes, generally thronged with sex workers, all lead through to Durga Charan Mitra Street, Sonagachi's main thoroughfare.

As you near the junction with Abinash Kaviraj Street, pick your way through the crush of pavement traders and their customers to the end of the Street where it meets Durga Charan Mitra Street; this is the heart of Sonagachi.

Turning right into Durga Charan Mitra Street, this long narrow thoroughfare will be pullulating with humanity. Throughout the day there will be hundreds of sex workers evident, standing or squatting, singly or in groups outside the leprous frontages of the shabby, decaying buildings lining either side of the Street and tucked away down blind turnings.

I have heard it said that the area that is Sonagachi, accommodates an estimated ten thousand sex workers. This seems rather on the high side given the relatively small geographical area involved. Other estimates of five to six thousand sound more realistic although I have no idea how you would go about arranging any sort of reliable census.

The sinister and to me very disturbing aspect to all this, is that many of these ladies, both the young and not so young, will have been trafficked into prostitution. I have seen figures suggesting that five thousand girls go missing every day in India; the implication being that a percentage of these will end up being trafficked. Whilst this at first seems an impossible figure, is it really? In a country with a population approaching 1.3 billion, a figure of five thousand seems horribly and frighteningly insignificant.

Another thing that strikes you as you make your way westwards down the Street, is just how many of the ladies are seemingly from India's north east States or from Nepal. How had they come to be here unless trafficked? This was confirmed to me by my friend Udita Chatterjee, who as an NGO professional had at one time been involved in running programmes to provide safe areas for women vulnerable to trafficking or who had already been trafficked. She told me that one of the main reasons stemmed from the degree of rural poverty in these areas but another was the lighter skin colour of women from these parts which made them particularly valuable to the traffickers. I also learned from her that many girls who are trafficked from poor villages, either within India or across the borders in Nepal and Bangladesh, are often first enticed by people known and even related to them, an aunt or uncle for instance. Often this enticement involves false promises of marriage or jobs. When the girls are then trafficked into the cities they are sold into brothels or other exploitative employment.

There are a number of organisations working for the welfare of the sex workers of Sonagachi. For some of these organisations, the impetus has been promoting sexual health; preventing the spread of HIV and other sexually transmitted diseases, the 'Sonagachi Project' having been the forerunner.

The Project has developed over the years into a full blown cooperative run by the sex workers themselves. The success of the cooperative is that it has organised a majority of the sex workers in Sonagachi into a force with the influence to protect and promote their interests. These combined sex workers are not at all averse to picketing police stations demanding action against criminals operating on their patch. They have also been effective in combatting child prostitution by rescuing or reporting under aged girls, sold or duped into the trade. Cynics would say that the desired removal of the competition such under aged girls pose, is also a factor in such altruism. There may be something in that but so what if the end result is the same.

The Project also runs literacy classes for sex workers, those who are literate teaching the unlettered. There are also programmes for the children of sex workers, a clearly highly vulnerable group.

As you progress towards the end of the Street as it nears Rabindra Sarani and just before you reach the 'Chitpur Slaughter House', you will see to your right a highly ornate building. The frontage of this building boasts no fewer than nine pretty semi-circular balconies arranged over three floors; completely unexpected in this location. The ground floor of this building is taken up by the offices of 'Apne.app – Women Worldwide'. This charitable trust (www.apneapp.org) works to empower women to put an end to sex trafficking by increasing choices for the at risk groups. Founded 25 years ago by Ruchira Gupta, the organisation provides a very worthy service.

Just past the offices of 'Apne.app' and just to the side of a tiny Mosque, is the entrance to the small but bustling Allan Market. On entering the Market, fruit and vegetables are to the fore with meat and fish traders occupying the rear sections. In the far corner amongst the fish stalls, there is a tiny Hindu shrine and to the left of this a gateway. The gateway leads into a very narrow and grubby gullee which if you turn left, leads out into

Rabindra Sarani. This gullee has to rank as one of the most insalubrious spots in the area. All the festering buildings down the right hand side of the gullee are brothels; the doorways thronged with sex workers, some of an alarmingly young appearance. Those not crowding the entrances to buildings are squatting all over the gullee, particularly at its opening onto Rabindra Sarani. This place is disturbing enough in daylight; after dark it is hellish.

Back on Rabindra Sarani, turn left and take the next turning left into Garan Hatta Street. The Street follows a graceful curve to the right and contains numerous premises of dealers in precious and semi-precious metals and gems. Most of these premises include small workshops producing the items displayed in the shop front windows. The Street ends where it joins Beadon Street; officially renamed Dani Ghosh Sarani although I have yet to hear that new name used by any local.

Turning left into Beadon Street, cross over to the opposite pavement and walk past the Chactanya Library to your right until you reach the famous and historic Minerva Theatre. Built in 1873, the Minerva played an important part in the Bengali cultural renaissance, having a close association with the great playwright and actor, Girish Chandra Ghose. The Theatre underwent extensive refurbishment in 2007.

A little further on past the Minerva you reach the junction with Jatindra Mohan Avenue; the starting point. The Sovabazar Metro station, lies a ten minute stroll to your left. Girish Park Metro station is approximately the same distance to your right.

Chapter 11

RAM BAGAN

This walk takes you through Ram Bagan, an area which is to be found between Rabindra Sarani and Jatindra Mohan (JM) Avenue just south of Beadon Street.

Most of my Bengali friends and acquaintances in Calcutta will regard Ram Bagan as an insalubrious slum. There is no denying this but it is also an area of great vibrancy, inhabited by friendly and industrious people. It is certainly the sort of place (and there are many such others in Calcutta), where you can and often do, meet with the unexpected around every other street corner.

The starting point is the north western corner of the junction of CR Avenue and Vivekananda Road. It is at this point that northwards, CR Avenue becomes Jatindra Mohan (JM) Avenue. Fifty metres north of this junction is the Girish Park Metro station.

Keeping to the northern pavement, head westwards down Vivekananda Road. Here you encounter a very odd major civil engineering project. Your first sight of this is the gaping ends of a yet to be completed dual flyover. This takes up almost the entire width of the road with the flyover parapets so close to the second floor apartments of the buildings lining either side of the Road, that the inhabitants could quite easily open their windows stick out their arm and touch the structure; it simply has to be seen to be believed. Perhaps even less fortunate are those occupants living on the ground and first floors of the buildings; their view of the sky has been replaced by the underside of the flyover decks. The situation for residents is bad enough now; if the flyover is ever completed, it will be horrendous.

One spin off of all this is that the decks of the dual flyover provide shelter from the elements at ground level. There is already evidence of pavement settlements and informal retail enterprises springing up to take advantage of this. Who can blame them for their encroachment? The structure is serving no other useful purpose at present.

The flyovers come to an abrupt end in the air where Vivekananda Road meets Rabindra Sarani but continues again about thirty metres further on across the junction. It really is a most bizarre sight. To my certain knowledge, nothing has visibly advanced on this project for approaching three years. How they are going to join up all these truncated sections (if they ever do) will be something worth watching.

Turning right into Rabindra Sarani, you are immediately swept up in the unrelenting tumult always present in this frantically busy thoroughfare. There are trams, buses, lorries, taxis and rickshaws both hand pulled and motorised, all vying for passage through the congestion and chaos.

Keep over to the right hand pavement, picking you way carefully through all around you. You pass a small turning on your right into Gupta Lane then a little further on, a larger turning into Nanda Mullick Lane. At this point, look out for a small, tiled Hindu shrine, obstructing the pavement ahead of you, almost opposite number 297. Just a few metres past this shrine and almost lost amongst the groups of ladies congregating here, is the narrow entrance to Sett Bagan Gullee, you onward route into Ram Bagan.

Sett Bagan Gulley, barely two metres wide, is a notorious red light area. Depending upon the time of day, the entrance to and the first one hundred metres or so of the Gullee will be lined with sex workers standing or sitting outside the tiny doorways giving access to the teeming tenements beyond. As applies in Sonagachi, described in the last chapter, do not point cameras here; it will not be appreciated.

With the help of Sumona (not her real name), a female Calcutta contact familiar with this place and its people, I had made a tour of some of these tenements the year prior to my current visit. The initial surprise is just how much lies beyond each of the small doorways leading off the Gullee. You enter into a dimly or completely unlit, labyrinth of dank and filthy corridors, landings and half landings leading off this way and that, all connected by crumbling uneven and slippery brick stairways. There are people everywhere; drawing water from the communal pump; noisily washing pots and pans; soaping and scrubbing clothes on the flagstone floors; tending pots of vegetables and rice simmering over smoky dung fires. Whole families occupy tiny single rooms, some subdivided by a kind of mezzanine platform to increase useable space. Even the flat roofs have been packed tightly with tiny shanties constructed of boarding, tarpaulin and bits of tin. I tried in vain to make a rough tally of the approximate numbers occupying this tenement and quickly abandoned this as impossible. It would certainly not be an exaggeration to put a figure of between 100 and 120 souls occupying this one tenement concealed behind what outwardly, is a single entrance door off the Gullee. I toured several separate tenements all along the Gullee and found all much the same in terms of living conditions and overcrowding.

Nobody inhabiting these tenements can enjoy any real personal space and it is unlikely that there is any real concept of such. Life is conducted communally; there is no other choice.

One really lasting memory of all this was the complete lack of curiosity of any of the residents towards my presence amongst them. It cannot have been often, if at all, that a westerner had visited their building. Yet there I was wandering about their homes, peering into this and that asking questions through my contact and there was no one, except the children, who showed any sign at all that this was in any way unusual.

Although the Gullee is a red light area, I found no evidence from my tours of the tenement buildings of any of the sort of organised brothels one would find in Sonagachi just north of here. If indeed there is any organisation of the sex workers here then it is as low key as to be near invisible. From what I saw, the majority of the sex workers operating here are what may be termed freelance.

Treated respectfully, the ladies here are generally very good natured and quite ready to have fun at your expense by ribbing you with their extravagant invitations, many of which my contact was at first reluctant to translate for me. They also seem to have formidable memories. On my latest visit whilst researching this book and in the area, I was approached by three of the ladies who surrounding me, were passing comments back and forth amongst themselves whilst pointing at my eyes then their own eyes. I had no one to interpret at the time and it was only after much mutual misunderstanding, that I finally grasped, we had met before when more than a year before I had nosed around their tenement building with my contact.

As you get further into the Gullee, the visible red light activity begins to peter out but you still have the crowded tenements beyond the small low doorways leading off. Where you come to a sharp right hand bend in the Gullee, there is an extraordinarily noisy green parrot perched in its cage hanging just above head height. It is an evil tempered creature so keep your fingers clear of the cage bars.

Where the Gullee ends, turn left into Peary Das Lane. Keeping hard over to the left follow the Lane round until it emerges into Ramesh Dutta Street; the heart of Ram Bagan.

Turn left and follow Ramesh Dutta Street all the way down until it meets Rabindra Sarani. On the way there is much to gain your attention both in the Street itself and the numerous side lanes leading off. Metal bashing best sums it up. From everywhere your ears are assaulted by the sound of heavy hammers striking steel; shaping it, bending it and any number of other processes. There are sheets of steel piled everywhere, being cut with angle grinders and acetylene torches. Cut sections then being joined together with rivets and arc welders. The noise can be deafening particularly in the corrugated iron workshops of the by lanes.

The product of all this activity is piled outside the workshops; everything from domestic cooking pots and pans to huge industrial vessels and other containers. Many of the smaller domestic items can be found offered for sale in the numerous ironmongery retail outlets just around the corner in Rabindra Sarani.

Return back along Ramesh Dutta Street on the opposite (left) side of the thoroughfare. You will pass by a huge midden of assorted garbage, assiduously being picked over by scavengers, crows and street dogs. Surrounding and beyond this midden are a line of crude pavement shacks in which the scavengers live. They are fearful places.

Carry on walking eastwards along the Street, passing your original point of entry on your right. The Street bends to the left, becoming increasingly chaotic and grubby. Past this bend, over to the right is a housing scheme provided by the Dedra Bhartia Charitable Trust of Calcutta (according to the notice on the frontage of the building). Just left of this plaque is a walkway which will take you into the central courtyard of the housing scheme. It is worth a look as a good example of inner city social housing, vaguely reminiscent of London's Peabody and Guinness Trust developments.

Just before the Street emerges into JM Avenue, there is a premises to the right involved in the manufacture of near life sized models crafted in polystyrene and then expertly painted. There are Camels, Lions, Gorillas and Giraffes as well as well-known Hindu Deities such as Hanuman and Ganesh.

Once out into JM Avenue, turn right and your starting point and the Girish Park Metro station, are located a few blocks to the South.

Chapter 12

PATHURIAGHAT

This walk takes in the southern part of Jorabagan which is located between Nimtola Ghat Street and Pathuriaghat Street. To get the best out the market area you will pass through, the morning is the best time to visit.

The starting point is the south western corner of the junction of Rabindra Sarani with Beadon Street/Nimtola Ghat Street.

Walking southwards down Rabindra Sarani take the second turning on the right into Prasanna Kumar (PK) Tagore Street. This turning is almost directly opposite to the difficult to find entrance to Sett Bagan Gullee, visited in the previous chapter.

On entering PK Tagore Street, you meet with a frantically busy and congested market area. There are laden barrows and carts coming at you from all directions. The carriageway is narrow enough anyway but made more so by the overspill of sacks, boxes and crates from the numerous open fronted shop premises lining either side of the Street. It is a great place to stand, if you can find an unoccupied corner, just taking in all that is going on.

Just along to the left, is the narrow and perpetually crowded entrance to Pathuria Ghat Lane; a chaotic little thoroughfare which quickly meets the wider and relatively more sedate Pathuria Ghat Street. The reason for this brief diversion lies on the opposite side of the Street at number 57. Here is a fantastically ornamented, two storey residential building; one of the finest examples to be found anywhere in North Calcutta. The blue painted frontage incorporates a pair of well proportioned bays with balconies above. The parapet is adorned with a number of carved figures and, at ground level, the grand entrance door has an intricate pattern in tile work above it. Perhaps as surprising as finding such a building here at all, is that, from visual inspection it looks to be in excellent repair and very well maintained.

Retrace your steps back along the Lane to re-join PK Tagore Street. Turning left you pass a sizeable Hindu temple then enter an area of the market comprising numerous pavement sellers packed closely together along both sides of the Street. They trade mainly in foodstuffs; vegetables, fruit and assorted herbs and spices with all sorts of wet fish further along. On this visit I am disappointed at the absence of an elderly lady vegetable seller I had come to be on friendly terms with. Many years ago I took the lady's photograph and on my next visit handed her several prints for her use. On every subsequent visit I would seek her out at her pitch in the market to exchange greetings. It is a little concerning not to be able to find any trace of her on this visit.

There are some very surprising buildings along PK Tagore Street, one exceptionally so. To the left and set back a little behind the building line, is an enormous old mansion with six massive Corinthian columns incorporated into the magnificent frontage. The general effect is spoiled however, by the crude corrugated iron fencing marring the ground floor level. It is difficult to determine if this old mansion is still occupied or at least partly so. It is certainly very dilapidated and now possibly beyond economic restoration. There is a sign fixed to the rough iron gates at the entrance which reads 'Sreejit Kumar Tagore', presumably the owner and almost certainly a surviving member of the famous Tagore family of which Rabindranath, India's first Nobel Laureate, is possibly the best known to western travellers.

A little further on down the Street and over to the right, is what is left of one of the most unusual buildings ever to have graced Calcutta's built environment. You need to look upwards to spot it, for what remains at ground level has almost vanished, having been surrounded and suffocated by later development, much of it hideous and seemingly, illegal. What you will spot is 'Tagore Castle'; built in the mid nineteenth century by Jatindra Mohan Tagore and clearly influenced by his travels in Europe, particularly Scotland. The mix of architectural styles which went into this building is bewildering. Apart from the battlements, the weather vanes and the clock tower, there are stepped gables, oriel and arrow slit windows and balconies in several different styles. All in all a fantastical and very pleasing building or at least once it was. I have seen a 19th century engraving executed shortly after the completion of the Castle. It was magnificently eccentric in appearance; something out of a Scott novel or some fairy tale. Then of course it stood on its own, in splendid isolation, as it was meant to be viewed. Now you really have to use your imagination to get an idea of how it once looked.

A few visits back, I had an unofficial snoop around the interior of the Castle. At that time it had been illegally squatted for a number of years; indeed still was at the time I visited. The interior had been gutted of anything which had either beauty or value and a lot which must have formed part of the internal structural integrity of the building.

The current condition of Tagore Castle is truly deplorable, indeed an absolute disgrace. This is one of the buildings officially recognised and listed by the Calcutta Municipal Corporation as a 'Heritage Building' and one would have thought, subject to some protection. Even so, absolutely nothing has been done to preserve the Castle or even to arrest its decay. Worse still, no action has been taken to demolish the plethora of clearly illegal and ramshackle structures which have engulfed the Castle's lower levels, even where they have been physically tacked on to the Castle itself.

Sadly this is the altogether common pattern with many other of Calcutta's officially listed heritage buildings; inertia and wilful neglect. A pox upon whoever is responsible.

If you look carefully beyond the pavement traders at ground level you can pick out the massive gateposts and remains of the iron gates which originally gave access to the Castle. There are three pairs surviving but only one still retaining the actual gates.

Twenty metres or so on from the Castle and over to the left, is the old Metropolitan Institute, currently in use as the Pathuriaghat Post Office. Built in 1887 this once fine building is now in a very sorry state of repair.

Further on, over to the right and beyond the fish sellers, is another enormous old mansion; the frontage set off with eight giant fluted columns and statuary (sadly with only one statue remaining) at roof level. It is not clear what use this building currently serves but there are clearly two distinctly separate occupants. This is evident since one occupant, controlling the left hand side of the building has vandalised their half by painting the old stonework a garish shade of pinkie red. Why would anyone do this? Whatever possessed them?

Just beyond this vandalised and desecrated old mansion is a turning to the right into Baishnab Sett 1st Lane. This is a place like many from here on, where life spills out of the tiny dwellings onto the doorsteps and out into the carriageway, which of course is what makes it all so interesting. Just past a pair of urinals you come across a very strange sight. Over to the left, on a kind of forecourt to one of the tiny houses is just about the most dilapidated old car you will ever see. All four wheels vanished long ago and the rotted, rusted chassis and remaining body gives the appearance of having sunk disintegrating, into the concrete. Any paintwork there was has been scoured away by many Calcutta seasons. To my knowledge this wreck has been here for ten years although having consulted neighbours, I am told it is actually more than twenty years. It now seems to have become accepted as part of the streetscape. I have seen this ruin in use as children's play equipment, shelter for chickens and a convenient surface for drying laundry. It is a wonder it has not been carted off by scavengers for its metal content although I suspect they would not think it worth the effort, it being now more rust than metal.

At the end of the Lane is a small Hindu shrine and to the right of this is Braja Kumar Seth Lane. Here again most life is lived outside in the open. Residents of the grim buildings lining the Lane are sitting, squatting even laying sleeping out in the Lane; your passage past them providing a brief diversion for them.

Just where the Lane turns to the right, there is an enterprise dealing in dried cow dung; used widely throughout India as a fuel for cooking fires. It is fashioned into small flat cakes often with a hole in the centre to allow the finished product to be strung together in batches of twenty or more. I have even seen these made with a decorative design around the edges. The 'cakes' are then laid out in the sun to bake dry. At this point in the Lane you have to pick your way through the several hundred spread out everywhere.

The Lane soon merges into Tagore Castle Street. Despite the name, the main part of the Street offers no further views of the Castle. This is thanks mainly to the vile, four storey tenement flung up along the entire right hand side of the Street. Look out to your left for a building signed 'Bilotia Bhawan'. Directly opposite this building is an iron grill across an opening which is usually left open during daylight hours. Walking through brings you into what seems to be a kind of extension to the Street you have just left and where you can get further glimpses of what is left of the Castle.

A little further along, you can see that the whole of one of the Castle's flank walls has had tacked onto it numerous, hideous and presumably, illegal concrete extensions. These clearly did not just appear overnight yet no enforcement action seems to have been taken. Perhaps the sheer scale of unauthorised development in Calcutta has simply overwhelmed the system.

During this latest visit, while researching this book, I stood at this spot watching the most awfully crude brick 'wall' being flung up across the upper floor of one of the Castle's last visible, turreted corners. Poor old Jatindra; it is a mercy he cannot see what has happened to his edifice.

Tagore Castle Street re-joins PK Tagore Street just west of where you originally entered from Rabindra Sarani. To return to the starting point, turn left and the junction with Beadon Street/Nimtola Ghat Street is a few minutes' walk away.

Chapter 13

NIMTOLA GHAT

The Nimtola Ghat is one of Calcutta's designated burning ghats on the River Hooghly. There are others but Nimtola is the largest and almost certainly the oldest.

A good starting point is the south western corner of the junction of Rabindra Sarani and Sovabazar Street. The nearest Metro station is Sovabazar just a few minutes' walk eastwards along Sri Aurobinda Sarani (located opposite Sovabazar Street).

Walk westwards down Sovabazar Street in the direction of the River. On your left at number 92B is the magnificent old house of Butto Kristo Paul, well signed courtesy of the Municipal Corporation. This wonderful old heritage building is certainly eccentric in the architectural sense but hugely pleasing and very well preserved. The ground floor of the building is taken up by 'Butto Kristo Paul – Chemists and Druggists' (Mr Paul having been the founder of a multinational pharmaceutical firm). This is completely original and unspoiled, virtually unchanged from the day it was first opened for business.

Just past this magnificent building, take the first turning on the left into Bawari Tola Lane which then quickly joins Beniatola Street. Turn right here keeping hard over to the left hand side of the Street as it curves gracefully to the left. At number 24/2 can be found the 'Fair Price Shop' (prop. Joydeb Dutta). There are many similarly named shops throughout Calcutta's backstreets; not in the sense that they are part of some chain store group but simply that the allusion in the name to honest bargains has caught on as a marketing ploy.

When you reach a TMC national flag of India to your right, take the turning on the left into Sen Lane. This is another of those byways where the locals conduct life as much outside in the Lane than within their own four walls. I am particularly drawn to such places which provide the opportunity to get a glimpse of neighbourhood life up close.

About half way down the Lane is a 'Government Regulated Kerosene Oil Shop (prop. Rampa Gupta and others'). The traveller will find many such shops throughout Calcutta. Kerosene, widely used to fuel cooking stoves and, not infrequently, the cause of tragic domestic fires when the stoves explode, is considered an essential commodity and the price is therefore regulated.

Just past the Kerosene shop, Sen Lane turns sharply to the right and becomes Nather Bagan Street. This ancient and peaceful backwater contains some once very grand buildings. Number 13 is particularly good with fine highly decorative, semi-circular balconies to the frontage. The building opposite at number 14 is also notable although not in such a good state of repair. The neighbouring building although once significant, is almost completely derelict but seemingly, still inhabited.

Take the next turning on your left into Nather Bagan Lane. Here you are back with life lived outside; there will be a group of ladies gossiping and washing clothes at the communal standpipe; children playing the sort of games played by children the world over, and the usual collection of loungers simply sitting and watching whatever events there are, unfold.

The Lane comes to an end where it meets Ahiritola Street. Turn right here into this narrow congested thoroughfare which takes you all the way down to the River Hooghly. As you pass down the Street, to the right is a highly ornamented Hindu temple which appears to have fallen into disuse long ago. It was clearly meant to be noticed in some earlier age as you can still see traces of the bright purple paint with which it was once adorned.

Just past this disused temple, over to the right and set back a little from the edge of the Lane is a small collection of bustees; perhaps a dozen dwellings in all. These are simple but very different from the appalling pavement shacks mentioned in earlier chapters. These are obviously licensed; officially sanctioned by the Municipal Corporation and therefore not liable to being cleared away at an hour's notice.

A little further on and the Street meets the line of the Circular Railway at a vehicular crossing point. Cross over the tracks and you are in Strand Bank Road with the River immediately to your right and just short of the Ahiritola Ferry Ghat.

Turn left and walk past the ramp leading down to the Ferry Ghat and the adjoining bathing ghat. Over to your left and strung out either side of the Circular Railway tracks are some of the most appalling shanties to be seen anywhere in Calcutta. These dreadful shacks, constructed from salvaged junk and all packed tightly together in frightful squalor are possibly only surpassed in awfulness by those lining the banks of the Circular Canal near Chitpur Bridge, further north.

Just where this slum begins to peter out, you enter a stretch of Strand Bank Road which has almost the air of some pleasure fair. There are numerous sellers of flower garlands, all sorts of Hindu religious artefacts, fruit and other offerings and the inevitable street caterers and chai vendors. Crowds of people are moving purposefully this way and that; those walking out of the Road being replaced by equal numbers entering it. There are more beggars present than would seem usual, no doubt to take advantage of the milling crowds.

To the right is a long row of buildings stretching along the embankment. This is the Nimtola Burning Ghat. Close by the beginning of the line of buildings, there is a sizeable gateway beneath a largish blue sign written in Bengali script. This gateway leads through to the traditional cremation grounds and then on down to the River where the ashes of the bodies consumed by the flames are scattered Walking through the gateway towards the River, the platforms of timber, the traditional funeral pyres, on which bodies are placed for cremation, are to the left; to the right are a line of shallow cremation pits. This traditional form of cremation, with relatives of the deceased lighting the funeral pyre, is still widely in use; accounting for about ten percent of all the cremations carried out at Nimtola. The remainder are dealt with by the Municipal Corporation's electric furnaces, housed in the buildings just south of this point. These more modern facilities are currently being extended.

Those who handle the bodies to be cremated here (and indeed corpses in hospitals and morgues), are known as Doms and are considered by other Hindus to be an 'untouchable' caste.

Just past the crematoria buildings, cross the railway tracks and turn left into Nimtola Ghat Street. The Street begins with a few twists and turns before straightening out for most of the remainder of its length. Where the Street first bends to the right, is a kind of pavement soup kitchen for the poor, operated by one of the City's charitable bodies. Huge cauldrons of rice and great pots of dal are being stirred whilst the hungry stand patiently in line waiting to be served their portion on a banana leaf. It is just another of the many things the traveller will witness daily in the back streets of Calcutta which will make them count their blessings.

As you progress eastwards along Nimtola Ghat Street, you will pass numerous premises dealing in the timber used to fuel Nimtola's traditional cremation pyres.

The further east you walk along the Street the busier and more congested it becomes. By the time you cross the BK Paul Avenue junction the traffic is chock a block and the pavements thick with people. A little further on, close to the junction with Rabindra Sarani there is an eerie old building over to the left; a great windowless barn of a place, all columns and decaying fancy detail. This decrepit empty shell is the old Duff College, abandoned decades ago and now so structurally unsound that even squatters steer clear of the place. Every time I pass by I expect to see it collapsed into a pile of rubble.

When reaching Rabindra Sarani, you can return to the start point by turning left and taking a ten minute stroll northwards. Alternatively, you can carry on straight over Rabindra Sarani into Beadon Street and walk to the next main junction with Jatindra Mohan Avenue. From there the Sovabazar Metro station lies about five minutes' walk to the left whilst Girish Park Metro station is a roughly equal distance to the right.

Chapter 14

South East of BB Ganguly Street

This chapter deals with the area squeezed between Nirmal Chandra Street to the east, CR Avenue to the west and south of Bipin Behari (BB) Ganguly Street.

The starting point for this short walk is the south eastern corner of the junction of CR Avenue and BB Ganguly Street. This is close by the southern entrance to Central Metro station.

Walking southwards along CR Avenue you will pass by a whole colony of pavement dwellers, strung out from the Metro station entrance to way beyond the Yogayog Bhavan, about two hundred metres distant.

In my last extended visit to Calcutta whilst researching this book, I was lodging nearby this spot so came to know most of these pavement dwellers by sight and was on nodding terms with a fair number of them. It did not matter what time of the day or night I passed by, coming from or returning to my lodgings, I would see the same characters, more or less still exactly placed where you had last seen them. It never changed; they were as an immovable part of the street scene as were the lamp posts.

This set me wondering just how they passed their time; what did they do with their waking hours? You know how it is if you are forced to kill even half an hour; how quickly boredom sets in and how slowly the minutes pass. Yet there were these people simply sitting there hour after hour, day in day out, surrounded by their meagre worldly possessions. How did they tolerate the tedium of it all? It became almost an obsession with me; I would go out of my way to pass them by on my numerous comings and goings. I suppose the pattern of their lives was simply dictated by their circumstances, they having no real choices in the matter. This got me thinking that this utter tedium must be as equally intolerable as the material deprivation involved in this way of life.

Just past the Yogayog Bhavan, you come to a statue occupying a kind of island dividing a turning to your left into Malinga Lane. The statue is of Sarda Vallabbhai Patel (1875-1950), 'the Iron Man of India'. He was a barrister and statesman and one of the leading members of the Indian National Congress; now regarded as one of the founding fathers of the Republic.

As you turn left into Malinga Lane, note the interesting wedge shaped, yellow building to the right; an ingenious use of a restricted and compact plot.

Take the first turning to the right just by the premises of the 'Bengal Engineering Company'. A short way on, turn left into what is still, confusingly, Malinga Lane. In fact little chopped off sections of this old Lane can be found all over the immediate vicinity; yet another example of a once continuous thoroughfare dissected by subsequent development. Interestingly in most such cases, nobody usually bothers to renumber the scattered parts.

Malinga Lane is fairly narrow and in parts, also pretty grimy, particularly where it crosses Srimanta Dey Lane. The Lane twists first left then right, then narrows even further. At this point, look over to the left and spot the fine old cast iron bollard incorporating a public water tap. The barrel of the bollard boasts a beautifully cast Lion's head; a not uncommon piece of street furniture found in many of the older lanes from hereabouts, northwards to Baghbazar.

At number 27 Malinga Lane is a richly ornamented, three storey building of some significance. It is completely out of keeping with surrounding buildings, indicating that it predates its rickety neighbours and originally stood alone and uncluttered by them. The ground floor is occupied by 'Metal Craft – Efficient Craftsmanship on (sic) Metal'.

Opposite number 32/1, there is a turning to the left which is Halder Lane. This is marked by a rounded corner building, the upper level of which is garishly decorated in green and yellow stripes; not an easy building to miss.

Halder Lane is barely two metres wide; a winding quiet little backwater. Just where the Lane begins a turn to the left, there is the premises of the 'Malinga Athletic Club'. Just past here at number 7, notice the pair of ancient, carved entrance doors, now in urgent need of restoration.

This is the sort of neighbourhood where, if you are particularly lucky, you may catch sight of the old fashioned; 'bheestie' with his wooden yoke from which hang his goatskins containing fresh drinking water. These chaps really do still exist in Calcutta but in ever dwindling numbers. His customers will be Muslims as no Hindu would drink water 'contaminated' by animal skin.

At the end of the Lane, past a luridly painted, pink and blue house, turn left into Madan Baral Lane. The Lane swings right passing the premises of 'Bowbazar Chatterjee Memorial Welfare Society' at number 22/3A. Reaching number 45, the 'Unique Haircutting Saloon', turn right into Das Lane. Next door to number 16, is a quite remarkably ornate, red fronted building. It boasts three decorative arches above the first storey windows, nicely set off by three pretty ironwork balconies to the top storey.

At the end of this shortish Lane, turn right into Gopi Mohan Bose Road. You will pass to your left, 'St Joseph's College' and on your right, the 'Bliss Ladies' Beauty Salon' before reaching the junction with Fakir Dey Lane. Cross straight over this junction into the twisting Jadu Nath Dey Lane. The Lane snakes to the right then left before emerging into hectic Nirmal Chandra Street, the southern 'extension' of College Street.

On reaching Nirmal Chandra Street, turn left and a few minutes' walk takes you to the major junction with BB Ganguly Street. Just before the junction, look to your left down the intriguingly named Bowbazar Orphanage Lane; a tiny narrow thoroughfare leading westward but which, so far as I could discover, no longer contains any orphanage.

The major junction where Nirmal Chandra Street northwards becomes College Street and is crossed by BB Ganguly Street is, in a geometric sense, just about the very epicentre of Calcutta proper.

Turning left at the junction into BB Ganguly Street, cross to the opposite side of the Street. Here, at number 243, next door to 'Eastern Furnishers' is a small Hindu Temple of unusual and unique origin. This is the 'Firanghee Kali Bari', the foreigner's temple of Kali Ma. The foreigner concerned who had the Temple built, was an unusual 19th century Englishman by the name of Anthony Kabial. He joins those, such as the wonderfully eccentric 'Hindoo Stuart' (of whom more later), as among the few westerners of the age to fully embrace Hindu culture and religion.

A further few minutes' walk southwards down BB Ganguly Street brings you back the starting point, Central Metro station.

Chapter 15

KURMATOLI AND SOVABAZAR

A good starting point for this excursion is the north western corner of the busy junction of Jatindra Mohan (JM) Avenue with Sri Aurobinda Sarani (Grey Street as was), close by the Sovabazar Metro station.

If arriving at the starting point by Metro, take the exit marked 'NK Park'. This will bring you out on the correct side of JM Avenue.

Walk southwards along JM Avenue, taking the first turning on the right into Sri Aurobinda Sarani. On both sides of this thoroughfare there is a lot of recycling going on; here it is mainly sacks. Cement sacks, flour sacks, gram sacks; piles of them all over the pavement being sorted, bundled and stacked, all destined for reuse.

Just over to the left is a line of slum dwellings of the more permanent variety. The upper levels of these dwellings are absolutely festooned with ragged and faded laundry; the quantity indicating the considerable numbers of people who must be housed there.

Just past the junction with BK Paul Avenue and 'Dr Roy's Diagnostic Centre' you meet the northern reaches of Rabindra

Sarani. Immediately before reaching the junction, search out to your right the narrow entrance to the equally narrow and madly congested Raja Debendra Narayan Lane. Although tucked away off the back edge of the pavement, it is not so difficult to locate on account of the swarms of people entering and leaving, for this is the entrance to Sovabazar Market.

Joining the scrum, squeeze into the Lane and marvel at the huge amount of laundry strung out on high lines all along the left hand side. The lines are so high that the ladies use a kind of long cleft stick to place and retrieve the laundered garments. They need great skill to perform this operation as one slip and the freshly washed items fall into the muddy, vegetable waste strewn mess underfoot.

The entrance to the actual Market lies at the end of the Lane. As Calcutta markets go, Sovabazar's is remarkably neat and ordered. It is also largely under cover; a welcome relief if the sun is high. I like nosing around Calcutta's markets, crowded and noisy as they are, this one being no exception. Here the huge displays of herbs, spices, fruit and vegetables seems particularly artistic, even down to the strategic placing of all the different types, shapes and colours. I like the way the stock is periodically and surreptitiously sprinkled or sprayed with water to enhance the appearance of freshness.

Once you have had your fill of the Market, squeeze back down the Lane, turning right out into the junction. Cross over the junction, turning right into Rabindra Sarani and head along the left hand (western) pavement.

Although these are the northern reaches of Rabindra Sarani, it is still a busy trading thoroughfare. Look out for number 457 to the left; the premises of Mangal Basanalay, famous for its brassware.

The next turning on the left is Nandaram Sen Street with a large Hindu temple rising above the nearby buildings. This part of North Calcutta is particularly well served with new street signage. Perhaps the area has particularly good ward councillors with the energy to spur the Municipal Corporation into action. All the new signage along the main thoroughfares, such as this, is in both Bengali and English. In the side streets and lanes, the signage is in Bengali only. Getting around Calcutta would be a lot less bewildering to non locals if this sort of signage were to be extended across the City.

Over to the right at number 488 is the premises of 'Chandra Paul and Son – Sculptors in bronze, marble and fibreglass'. Examples of their skilful productions are stacked all over the pavement. At number 487 to the left is a workshop producing the wire and straw foundations of the Hindu deities used in Calcutta's many festivals. These frames will later be encased with clay by the potters (kumors) for which the area, Kumatoli, is famous (more on which shortly).

Over to the right is a largish, open fronted Hindu temple, painted bright red and usually thronged with those paying their devotions. To the left is usually to be found a sizeable community of pavement dwellers. Their livelihood seems to be derived from scavenging, judging by the piles of neatly sorted trash lining the pavement. This settlement, like many such others throughout the City, is of course illegal and liable to be cleared away at an hour's notice. When this happens, the colonies gradually start to reform, often in exactly the same location. What else can these people do? They must live somewhere.

Take the next turning on the left into Durga Charan Banerji Street, then twenty metres further on turn left again into Gopeswar Pal Street. Here is Kumatoli proper, comprising scores of often tiny, workshops and yards spread throughout twisting and winding lanes from here westwards towards the River Hooghly.

The small neighbourhood of Kumatoli has been renowned for its pottery and clay image making for more than two centuries. Most of the clay comes from the nearby River ghat and you will see great mounds of the stuff oozing wet, outside nearly every workshop and yard.

The 'Kumors' are kept busy producing images full time and throughout the year to cater for the many Bengali Hindu festivals of Calcutta. Their product is in demand not just locally but in other cities of India and abroad.

Walking down Gopeswar Pal Street you pass lines of clay images in all the various stages of construction, from the initial straw and wire framework to those freshly encased in clay, left standing in the sun to dry and those being skilfully painted and decorated by the specialist craftsmen. Most of the images are clearly recognisable Hindu deities, others less so, to me at least.

After fifty metres or so, the Street crosses Kumatoli Street. You can turn right here and wander all the way down and back taking in all the industry going on. Apart from the full figure images, you will see legs, arms, heads all set out to dry and harden in the sun. You could quite easily spend a few hours wandering the surrounding lanes casting an eye over it all.

Retracing your steps back along Kumatoli Street, the continuation of Gopeswar Pal Street is the second turning on the right. Walk right to the end and just before the Street meets Banamali Sarkar Street, you pass a workshop over to the right, which seems to specialise in giant size images. Some of these images are so huge that the craftsmen have to erect scaffolding from which to work on them.

Just at this point is another of those once grand old mansions dotted about here and there in the neighbourhood. This one, although certainly dilapidated, still appears reasonably sound.

Sadly, many of the others still standing, are in a far worse state of repair.

Turning right into Banamali Sarkar Street and following its twists and turns, you come to a small yellow painted Hindu shrine on the right. Opposite at number 36 is an appallingly ruinous, three storey house. Its special feature is a sizeable tree growing out of its flank wall at second storey level. The bulge this has caused to the front elevation is truly alarming, yet it is still apparently inhabited.

The Street swings sharp left then right, passing the 'Royal Sporting Club' at number 27A. Opposite is yet another once grand old mansion; this one being dated 1915 on its central raised parapet. There is a notice on the frontage indicating that the property has been acquired for development, so the arrival of the wreckers' ball cannot be far off and then it will be lost forever.

Past this point, the Street narrows to little more than a lane. Follow this down all the way until it meets the tracks of the Circular Railway. Cross the tracks into Strand Bank Road with the River and Champatola Ghat to your right.

All along each side of the railway track are living communities of ragpickers and other scavenging trades. There are lines of frightful, tightly packed makeshift shacks with tribes of ragged or near naked children playing in the filth outside and not a sign of even the most basic of amenities; no one should have to live like this.

A little further along Strand Bank Road you arrive at a ramp over to the right. This leads down to the landing stage of the Sovabazar Ferry Ghat, a stop on the Baghbazar to Howrah river ferry route.

Approximately thirty metres past the ramp to the ferry ghat and over to the left is the beginning of Sovabazar Street. Walking eastwards along the Street, with the River behind you, gives you the feeling of stepping back in time. From the railway tracks, the Street is lined with the frontages of old godowns and workshops which look as if they have not be touched since the day they were built here, most likely in the last quarter of the nineteenth century.

Further east, the Street hosts a kind of informal pavement market which you have to pick your way through carefully, without treading all over the fish, vegetables and whatever else is being hawked.

Crossing the junctions, first with Rabindra Sarani then BK Paul Avenue, brings you back to the start point at JM Avenue and Sovabazar Metro station.

Plate 1 Howrah Bridge

Plate 2 Mullick Ghat Flower Market

Plate 3 Rabindra Sarani/Colotolla Street Crossing

Plate 4 Hari Ram Goenka Street

Plate 5 Bow Bazar, BB Ganguly Street

Plate 6 Royd Street/Elliot Road Crossing

Plate 7 Sun Yat Sen Street

Plate 8 Nirmal Chandra Street

Plate 9 Lal Dighi and Central Post Office

Plate 10 MG Road

Plate 11 Dharmatala Street

Plate 12 Knifegrinder, Baithakkhana Lane

Plate 13 Zakaria Street

Plate 14 Bow Bazar, by Sealdah Flyover

Plate 15 MG Road/Chiteranjan Avenue Crossing

Plate 16 Victoria Memorial Hall

Chapter 16

BAGHBAZAR (EAST)

This particular foray is best undertaken on a Sunday; the only day of the week when the market at Galiff Street operates. The market is unique in Calcutta and it would be a pity to visit this part of Baghbazar without seeing it.

A good starting point is the south eastern side of the Chitpur (Chitpore) Bridge. This lies at the northernmost end of Rabindra Sarani where it meets with Kshirode Vidya Vinode Avenue (this being the northern extremity of the CR Avenue/JM Avenue/Girish Avenue main north south thoroughfare).

Walk to mid span on the Chitpur Bridge where you can get the best view of both banks of the Circular Canal, looking eastwards. Strung out along and packed tightly together on each bank are hundreds of terrible slum shanties. Inured as I am by now to Calcutta's worst excesses, to me these still represent the most appalling human habitation to be found anywhere in Calcutta. It may be the sheer scale of the slum or its setting along the festering muddy banks of this filthy waterway, but it is dreadful to contemplate the lives of those unfortunate enough to have to live here. I have no information as the numbers living here but it has to be in the thousands. The foul shacks making up this towering mess are packed several

BAGHBAZAR (EAST)

deep, some almost on the high tide mark of the rank waters of the Canal.

Along the low water mark of the Canal are a number of tiny square structures on stilts, roughly enclosed with old scraps of tarpaulin. These are the 'toilets' serving the slum dwellers; reliant on the small tidal movements of the Canal to remove the waste to deeper water. If as I tried, you attempt to roughly compute just how many residents have to share each of these primitive privies, you quickly give up in despair. I have never counted more than eight to ten of these amenities on stilts so each must serve literally hundreds of souls.

This sort of scene is not something you can ever get used to. Whenever I cross the Chitpur Bridge and witness all this it reminds me that much the same scene met me here on my arrival in Calcutta more than forty years ago. Then it was mainly refugees displaced from East Pakistan (now Bangladesh); today it is economic migrants from neighbouring States like Bihar and Orissa as well as illegals from over the border with impoverished Bangladesh. In all those intervening years I have never known any appreciable time when such a scene did not meet you from the Bridge.

Back at the southern end of the Bridge, turn left into Galiff Street which follows the line of the Canal eastwards. If you have come here on a Sunday, the Street will be crowded, for it is market day. This market specialises in plants and pet creatures, including all kinds of tropical fish and small amphibians.

The first section of the Market is mainly concerned with potted garden plants; everything from herbs to large ornamental varieties. The animal and tropical fish sections start a little further along. There are ladies with netted baskets of day old fluffy chicks, cages of mature chickens and cockerels, various songbirds and budgerigars (very popular in Calcutta), along with loudly squawking green parrots.. There is even a section for pigeon fanciers with ringed homing pigeons being traded for surprisingly large sums. There are kittens, cats, puppies, dogs, rabbits, mice and white rats. In the fish section there are tanks full of all sorts of exotic species. There are goldfish of every description and even tanks of tiny terrapins.

Mixed up in all this melee, are traders in pet requisites, aquarium apparatus and accessories, indeed everything the Bengali pet lover may require. There is no other market like this anywhere else in Calcutta and it has been operating for as long as I have known the City and very likely a great deal longer.

As you progress down Galiff Street, through the Market, you keep getting glimpses of the Canal slum settlements, through breaks in the buildings to your left. Over to the right, you pass by the Baghbazar tram terminus; the trams clanking to and fro up and down the Street.

Just past the tram terminus, take the first turning on the right into Akhoy Bose Lane, then almost immediately right again into Maratha Ditch Lane (appearing in the archaic form of Marhatta Ditch Lane on the old cast iron street nameplate). The origins of this street name lie in the extensive but ultimately ineffective eastern line of defence for eighteenth century Calcutta. The ditch, designed to protect Calcutta from the landward side, from marauding Marathas, was excavated between 1740 and 1742 but never fully completed. It ran from just north of this point all the way to the bottom (southern) end of present day Chowringhee.

Passing straight on down the entire length of Maratha Ditch Lane, you pass through two teeming junctions and past numerous tiny side streets and blind turnings. When you reach the lower end of the Lane, just before it ends at Nandalal Bose Lane, you pass an enormous and ornate old building with an unusual castellated parapet. Like so many other such once fine buildings, this one has been sorely neglected and is now is in a bad state of repair.

Turning left into Nandalal Bose Lane and about half way down its length is another of North Calcutta's once grand mansions. Now in a ruinous state, it has a parapet adorned with Grecian urns and highly ornate capitals to the four large brick columns on the frontage. One day the State Government will shake of its inertia and wake up to the once rich but now crumbling architectural heritage of the City. By then perhaps it will be too late to save what is left.

Where Nandalal Bose Lane ends at Baghbazar Street, turn left passing the St John Ambulance Association's 'Calcutta Sisir Kumar Institute Centre'

Keeping to the left hand side of the Street, turn left just past 'Roy's Jewellers' into a lane which still calls itself Baghbazar Street. Dead ahead at number 65/2 is 'Basubati', the house of Pasupati Bose and Nandalal Bose. This is a magnificent old mansion now all but derelict but apparently still occupied, in part at least. This is an important, officially listed 'heritage' building and it is a tragedy that it has been allowed to fall into such a state of disrepair as perhaps to be now beyond the possibility of restoration.

Retracing your steps back to Baghbazar Street proper and opposite the 'Ramakrishna Pharmacy', cross the Street into Bishwakosh Lane. Bishwakosh (encyclopaedia in Bengali) Lane commemorates Nagendranath Basu (1866-1938), a scholar who lived here. He compiled a twenty two volume Bengali encyclopaedia; a task which occupied twenty years of his life.

At the end of Bishwakosh Lane, turn right into Santi Ghosh Street. Note the mad tangles of external electrical wiring hanging from the frontages of some of the buildings here. This narrow winding old thoroughfare, full of crumbling buildings, turns sharply to the left before ending at Brindapan Pal Lane. Turn right here and follow the Lane the short distance southwards until it meets busy Bhupen Bose Avenue. Turn left here and about twenty metres on, you come to an entrance to the Shyambazar Metro station.

For those with a little more energy, if you carry on past the entrance to the Metro station and a little further east brings you to the Five Point crossing. This madly busy crossing is so called as it forms the convergence of five major thoroughfares; Bidhan Sarani, to the north and south, Bhupen Bose Avenue to the west, RG Kar Road to the east and APC (Upper Circular) Road to the south east.

Set in spectacular prominence in the centre of the crossing is the mounted statue of Subhas Chandra Bose or 'Netaji', meaning respected leader and one of India's national heroes.

Chapter 17

BAGHBAZAR (WEST)

As with the previous chapter, the Chitpur Bridge is a convenient starting point from which to explore the western arm of Baghbazar.

From the western side of the Bridge (facing the River Hooghly), you have a fine view of the Chitpur Lock, a marvel of Victorian engineering and still fully functioning. From the Bridge, head southwards, crossing the Galiff Street/Kshirode Vidya Vinode Avenue junction. At this point there is often a mobile dispensary unit operated by the NGO 'Calcutta Rescue'. The unit comprises a large van supplemented by an awning complete with benches. Medicines are dispensed to those too poor to pay for them. Many of the patiently queueing will have come from the appalling Canal side slums nearby or the bustees dotted about from here to Baghbazar Street.

Once across the junction, turn right then take the first turning on the left into NK Saha Lane. There is a small Hindu Temple on the left which incorporates an aviary of loudly cheeping budgerigars. Over to the right is a line of rudimentary street catering enterprises; almost obligatory in any Calcutta street scene. Cross over the Lane and take the first turning on the right into Dispensary Lane; an antique, narrow thoroughfare of simple single storey houses. Most of the inhabitants will be out of doors in the Lane; washing clothes, collecting water, preparing vegetables and gossiping amongst themselves; a jolly scene.

At the end of Dispensary Lane, turn left into Ram Krishna Lane. A similar scene greets you here; everything is going on out in the Lane itself. There are lots of children in evidence and numerous chickens getting under your feet as you make your way through. Interestingly, just about every other house seem to have a caged parrot hanging outside ready to squawk loudly at passers by.

Just past the junction with Durga Charan Mukherji Street, turn right into Ananda Neogy Lane. The Lane is a quiet backwater containing many of the traditional three, four and even five storey residential buildings, typical of this part of North Calcutta. A number boast interesting entrance doors; numbers 3 and 4B being good examples. Nearly all have the old louvered wooden shutters to all windows on the frontages.

At the end of the Lane is the northernmost reach of Rabindra Sarani. Turn left here and just past a brickworks cum builders' merchants, take the first turning on the left into a quiet and unnamed by lane which returns you to Rama Krishna Lane. As you leave this by lane, look over to your left at number 26 Rama Krishna Lane. There cannot be a more derelict yet still inhabited building anywhere in the City, at least one that is still substantially standing. Over to the right at number 23 is something very different. An amazingly ornate building with turrets and fancy parapet. Its neighbour at number 22 is also pleasing with a very pretty central, stone and ironwork balcony, set above a decorative entrance door.

The end of Rama Krishna Lane, joins the western arm of Baghbazar Street about mid way along its length. There is

BAGHBAZAR (WEST)

a lively street market here, well worth a brief diversion. Turn right and walk the fairly short distance westwards towards the River. The market is spread out on both sides of the Street; numerous fruit and vegetable sellers and a thriving trade in live chickens. Behind the market stalls are tightly packed shop premises, most quite tiny, some little more than cubby holes. If any of these shops still have their shutters down, note the number of padlocks applied. Four or five is not unusual; I have counted as many as nine fist sized locks before now. They take their security seriously hereabouts.

Towards the end of the Street, where it crosses the tracks of the Circular Railway, there once stood 'Perrins Redoubt'. This was a small, square fortification; a defensive outpost, remote from the British stronghold at the old Fort William, several kilometres to the south. Here on 16th June 1756, a small contingent of troops of the East India Company held out against an assault by several thousand of the Nawab, Siraj-Ud-Daula's troops.

The ground in front of this fortification had once been known as 'Perrin's Garden', Calcutta's most fashionable pleasure garden where it was 'the height of gentility for the (East India) Company's covenanted servants to take their ladies for an evening stroll or moonlight fete.' This hotspot went into decline following the laying out of 'The Park' around Lal Dighi at present day Dalhousie Square. Perrin's Garden was sold in 1752 and later used as a site for the manufacture of gunpowder.

Retracing your steps back along Baghbazar Street, just past the point you entered the Street, turn right into Kali Prasad Chakraborty Street. You pass, on your left, one of the City's many 'Ration Shops' and just where the Street bends right, the 'Gaudiya Mission'. The Mission is housed in the highly ornate and intricately detailed 'Sri Gaudiya Math' (Temple); an officially listed heritage building and in an excellent state of preservation.

Follow this ancient, meandering Street almost to the end where it begins to narrow considerably. Here, opposite a small printing works is a residential building to make you smile. The front elevation of this building has skilfully and quite artistically worked reliefs set in the smooth rendering at ground floor level. There are Hindu deities, including Shiva and Ganesh but also Micky Mouse, Donald Duck, Minnie Mouse and other Disney characters. Wonderfully eccentric!

At the end of the Street, turn left re-joining Rabindra Sarani, then twenty metres on, left again into Nivedita Lane. The name of the Lane commemorates Sister Nivedita who started her famous school for girls in 1898. Born Margaret Elizabeth Noble, Sister Nivedita was an Anglo Irish social pioneer, author and teacher. A disciple of Swami Vivekananda, he gave her the name Nivedita, meaning one dedicated to God. She worked tirelessly to improve the life of women of all castes and in later life embraced the cause of Indian nationalism. A remarkable lady.

Nivedita Lane was previously called Ramakanta Bose Street and is generally still known as such, being for the most part signed accordingly; very confusing unless you are aware of this.

The Lane (or Street if you prefer), leads out into Girish Avenue (this being the third stage of the continuous north/south artery which begins as Chitteranjan (CR) Avenue, becomes Jantindra Mohan (JM) Avenue, then Girish Avenue and finally Kshirode Vidya Vinode Avenue – all thanks to the mania for renaming.

As you turn into Girish Avenue, there is a curiously sited old house forming a kind of island in the centre of the carriageway. This is the one time home of Girish Chandra Ghose (1844 – 1912), from whom the Avenue (and Girish Park further south), takes its name. An accomplished Bengali actor, poet, playwright, author and musician, he was a flamboyant character, rumoured to have been something of a libertine in his younger days. The building is in fact only part of the original house, the remainder having been demolished with the laying out of the Avenue in the 1930's.

To return (should you need) to the starting point, head north past the old Ghose house and walk straight on until you see Chitpur Bridge.

Chapter 18

COLLEGE STREET – 'BOI PARA'

College Street and environs is regarded as the intellectual heart of Calcutta; a centre of learning and culture and the location of a number of respected academic institutions.

The College Street area is often referred to as Boi Para or book neighbourhood, famous for its bookshops, publishing houses and most of all, its hundreds of secondhand book stalls. Unusually for Calcutta, the place does not really get into full swing until about 10.30 to 11.00 am; so time your visit accordingly.

A good starting point is the north eastern corner of the now familiar and busy junction of CR Avenue and MG Road. Heading eastwards along MG Road you will see over to the right a number of headquarters premises of various musical bands, the pavements outside of which are usually thronged with resting bandsmen in the full regalia of their respective bands. Often as not this scene is complimented by the sounds of band practice taking place within the open fronted premises. These bands will be seen all over Calcutta at weddings, festivals and other celebrations. Some are very accomplished; others less so.

Keeping to the left hand (northern) pavement, you pass by numerous small scale catering enterprises, various pavement hawkers trading in shoes, umbrellas, miscellaneous hardware and newspaper and magazines. You will find goats, often in substantial numbers, tethered to the pavement railings along with bundles of leaves provided for their sustenance. Street dogs will be nosing in the rubbish strewn gutters with sometimes a roaming cow or two getting in everyone's way. On your left, you pass a number of narrow, noisy and congested side lanes, all leading into the pullulating Mechua Bazar area.

The next major junction is that where College Street runs north to south across MG Road. Pause for a while here and try to spot the brown shirted, duty 'Tram Points Man'. These chaps, employed by the Calcutta Tramways Company (CTC), are responsible for manually switching the tramline points so as to ensure the correct routing of passing trams. Watch as a number 11 tram comes clanking southwards down College Street. Once spotted the 'Tram Points Man' suddenly appears (I have never discovered where from) with his crowbar like implement. Defying the traffic he strides to the centre of the carriageway, inserts the iron bar in the tram track points, switching their direction thereby sending the oncoming tram on a right turn down MG Road. You will find these chaps at busy junctions all over Calcutta wherever trams still run.

Standing at the junction, the very large and as yet unfinished structure to your left is the new(ish) College Street Mall. This ongoing project occupies the site of the ancient College Street Market. Now partly occupied, the Mall when completed, will house many of the local booksellers. If you look closely at the iron railings running along the frontage of the Mall, you will see they incorporate a design detail depicting and open book in front of an outline of several human forms; a nice touch.

Directly opposite the College Street frontage of the Mall are a range of old buildings which have seen better days. Look up (something one must always do in Calcutta) and spot the one which has a pair of those traditional drama masks worked in stone on the upper level of the frontage. An ancient and long defunct theatre perhaps?

Cross to the south eastern corner of the junction and just past the statue of Kristodas Pal Bahadur, (one time Secretary of the British Indian Association), turn left into Bankim Chatterjee Street. On entering the Street, immediately to your left is the entrance to the famous College Street Coffee House. This was the one time haunt of young Bengali intellectuals and radicals although I am sure the current and largely student, clientele would also claim such description. The coffee, at least to my tastes, is spectacularly mediocre.

This busy little street is crammed with booksellers and stationers and there is quite often some sort of student demonstration going on; in solidarity, I have signed many a petition of theirs, written entirely in Bengali and therefore incomprehensible to me. Over to the right is the well reputed Hindu School and Sanskrit College.

Take the second turning on your right into Ramnath Mazundar Street. Opposite the small Hindu Temple to your right, sorely in need of a repaint, is a wonderful old mansion. Ornate stone balconies to all the upper three storeys and an imposing entranceway. All this set behind grand gateposts and noble iron railings.

A little further along the Street and to your right, is a large and garishly yellow painted building. Here the Street narrows considerably and turns sharply to the left. Your route lies straight ahead into Chintamoni Das Lane. This quiet little backwater is relatively free of traffic and offers a welcome if brief respite from the bedlam you have just left and will shortly re-join.

Just where the Lane ends, turn sharp left into Patuatola Lane. This ancient winding lane contains a number of traditional domestic buildings with highly decorative ironwork to their balconies. Where the Lane meets a tee junction, turn left. This is still Patuatola Lane, just a different branch of it. Follow the Lane as it curves round to the right before emerging out into MG Road.

Turn right into MG Road and less than one hundred metres on, you reach the junction with Amherst Street (Ram Mohan Roy Sarani as it is now officially known). Turn right into Amherst Street and walk the short distance to the next junction with Surya Sen Street. At this junction and over to the left is the singularly uninviting 'Durga Hotel'. Opposite the Hotel is a walled tip, generally crawling with ragpickers and other scavengers rummaging through the piles of trash.

Turn right into Surya Sen Street and head westwards. This is a hectic thoroughfare, linking Amherst Street with College Street and taking a great deal of through traffic. It is best to keep over to the right hand pavement.

Everything is going on in the Street; people bathing and laundering at the standpipes; shopkeepers creating clouds of dust and debris by 'sweeping' the pavements in front of their premises. Other shopkeepers armed with those curious implements comprising a stick with a duster like rag fixed to the tip, will be flapping away, and furiously rearranging the dust over their displays of goods.

In India and particularly in Calcutta, it has always struck me that there is a curious disconnection between effort expended and value of end result. It was in this Street that I once stood for a good quarter of an hour mesmerised by a prime example of this. On that occasion, there were two men; one armed with one of those single handed twig brooms, the other with a bucket of filthy water and a slimy rag. Their task in hand was the 'cleaning' of a set of wide steps leading up to the entrance of some commercial offices. Bucket man began swabbing the lower steps with his filthy water. His colleague commenced with the sweeping of the upper steps. They passed each other mid-flight. The end result was that the steps were noticeably filthier than when they began the task. This did not matter; the broom had been wielded; the filthy water sloshed – the task had been completed.

It will be evident by now that this little excursion has followed a kind of elongated rectangular route which is now returning you to College Street, just a little further south from where you left it earlier. As you near the end of Surya Sen Street you see to your right the open aspect of College Square; a pleasant and relatively peaceful public open space complete with open air swimming pool.

Where the Street meets the junction with College Street, turn right. Here both pavements of the thoroughfare and most side turnings are tightly packed with hundreds of second hand book stalls, the stock spilling over onto the pavements. Some of the book stalls are tiny, not much more than a cubby hole, others much larger and dealing with both second hand and new books. There are books on almost every conceivable subject to be found here and it is perhaps the only place in the entire City where traders seem content to let potential customers browse unmolested and at leisure without strident imprecations to purchase. It is said that occasionally, rare books are unearthed here among the tottering piles of the tattered mundane.

There are some fine and noble buildings along this stretch of College Street, housing the academic and medical institutions which abound hereabouts. There is the local campus of Calcutta University, the Presidency College, the Hindu College and the

COLLEGE STREET — 'BOI PARA'

Hare School. A little further south is the sprawling complex of the Medical College and Hospital.

Just past the Presidency College you return to the College Street/MG Road crossing. Turn left into MG Road and the start point is a ten minute walk westwards.

Chapter 19

BAITHAKKHANA

In the mid eighteenth century, the whole thoroughfare leading from present day Lalbazar to where Sealdah Railway Station now stands, equating roughly to the line of BB Ganguly Street and environs, was known by the name, Baithakkhana.

This took its name from an ancient Banyan Tree at the eastern extremity which formed a 'baithakkhana' or resting and meeting place for merchants and their caravans. This great Banyan Tree is actually noted on the earliest maps of Calcutta. It seems to have been located about the point where the present day Sealdah flyover crosses the easternmost extremity of BB Ganguly Street. Popular legend has it that this was the tree in whose shade Job Charnock would sit to conduct business with the merchants. The tree supposedly, was cut down with the laying out of the Circular Road in the early years of the nineteenth century.

There was also another route to Baithakkhana; this one from 'Black Town'; the native area of Calcutta in the eighteenth and early nineteenth centuries. Today, this is marked by Baithakkhana Road, running from Keshab Sen Street, southwards all the way to BB Ganguly Street just short of the Sealdah Flyover; a good stretch of it still a thriving market area.

BAITHAKKHANA

The starting point for this exploration is the south eastern corner of the busy MG Road/Amherst Street junction. Walking south eastwards along MG Road, brings you quickly to the junction with Surya Sen Street. Here you will see a number of makers of rubber stamps and all sorts of nameplates and office signage. You will also see some of the dwindling number of Calcutta's pavement letter writers with their old fashioned manual typewriters perched on upturned crates or wobbly fold up tables. For a nominal fee they will formulate letters from the information provided by their, often unlettered, clients or complete any number of the plethora of official forms which are the lifeblood of Indian bureaucracy. There used to be many more of these letter writers; found all over Calcutta's streets and particularly near major post offices, public offices like courts and in the commercial centres. The onward march of technology in the form of the mobile phones and sophisticated electronic information and cash remittance services is rapidly putting paid to these chaps' trade and it cannot be far off when they will vanish from Calcutta's streets altogether.

Crossing the junction, keep to the right hand pavement. All along this part of the Road there are numerous stationers specialising in wedding invitations and the like. They are particularly thick on the ground as you pass under a kind of colonnaded arcade where lots of what is on offer is on display. The Bengali wedding invitation is generally, a very grand sort of document with lots of gold lettering and artistic flourishes. The last one I received was about A4 size and on card so stiff and robust that it could not be folded or rolled and had to be taken along to the wedding in a carrier bag.

When you see, over on the opposite side of the Road, the 'Ideal Lodge' and 'Hotel Cozy' (sic), take the next turning on your right. This is Baithakkhana Road. As you enter this ancient, twisting commercial thoroughfare, the Sarendranath

College is over to the right and a little further on, to the left is a small Mosque painted bright pink.

There is trading going on everywhere you cast your eye. From shops, stalls and the pavement and in side lanes; every imaginable commodity being offered for sale. Goods are being moved to and fro, up and down the Road on carts, barrows and perched on heads, all weaving through the motorised traffic and throng of pedestrians.

At number 19 on the left, is the 'MegaCity Guest House', next door to the 'Darpan Guest Home'. Straight ahead is the 'Ananda Boarding House Lodge'; all grim looking places and definitely accommodation of last resort. I have found as a general rule in India, it is as well to steer clear of any hotel type establishment which has 'Home', 'Lodge', 'Tourist', 'De-Luxe' or, worst of all, 'Paradise' included in its title; such places being invariably frightful billets. Just past these shabby establishments, the Road narrows and the section of the market dealing mainly in spices begins; clearly evident from the medley of pungent aromas filling the air.

Off to the left, the market overspills into numerous tiny side lanes which, time allowing, are well worth exploring. Look out also for the Shaanwalla, a regular sight in this area. The Shaanwalla is the itinerant knife grinder who tours areas such as this in search of clients. He carries strung to his back, a contraption which looks very much like a folding unicycle. Once he secures a commission, his apparatus is unfolded and set up. The cycle wheel drives a grinding stone and the Shaanwalla sits showering passers by in sparks from whatever it is he is sharpening. His more mobile brother in trade will have an actual pedal bicycle to get him about from place to place. This is raised on a stand and pedalled to drive the grinding wheel through a system of pulleys and belts connected to the rear wheel.

BAITHAKKHANA

The further you travel along the Road, the more congested it becomes until finally, it spills out into BB Ganguly Street, just short of the Sealdah Flyover and opposite the Church of our Lady of Dolours. The Church has a pleasing clock tower with a clock which for some reason is perpetually fifty minutes fast. I have never known it to be any different.

Turn left into BB Ganguly Street and walk straight ahead to where the Street dips under the Sealdah flyover. Emerging the other side you will see a long orange and green painted building to the left. This is Sealdah, Calcutta's second main railway station. The Station is well worth a look even if only to soak up the atmosphere of the place and to witness the tides of people arriving and departing.

Back under the Sealdah flyover, you will see that the space beneath the flyover deck has been put to good use, serving as a covered market, selling a bewildering variety of goods. All this spills over onto the pavements and into the side lanes running parallel to the Flyover.

Once back out into BB Ganguly Street itself, walk westwards keeping to the left hand pavement. In the carriageway and all over the pavements are numerous fruit and vegetable hawkers, nearly all ladies. There will be those selling just, say onions or potatoes or herbs. Others will be trading in a variety of produce. Customers mill around the hawkers rigorously inspecting the freshness and quality of what is being offered; poking squeezing or smelling the goods. Where, as is mostly the case, the produce is sold by weight,, a pair of ancient hand held scales will be produced; iron weights placed one side, the purchase on the other. Crude but effective.

Spread out within and behind the buildings to your left is a huge wholesale vegetable market. Fantastically laden coolies will be emerging from this market by narrow passageways between the buildings, dumping their loads into the backs of buyers' trucks. Often they will reburden themselves with loads from other waiting trucks, returning back to the market to replenish stocks. A good place to watch all this activity is the market access lane directly opposite Ghosh and Co. at number 156 and another about ten metres further along. You can also access the market at these points but be prepared to leap out of the way of heavily laden coolies emerging. Within the wholesale market it is completely chaotic. You hardly dare stand still for a second for fear of being knocked off your feet by the milling crowds.

Back out in the Street, you will witness the lifting of unbelievable loads onto the heads of waiting coolies. A regular sight will be four or five coolies jointly lifting and placing an enormous basket of produce on the head of one of their comrades who, by strength and a miracle of balance, transfers this to wherever it is required. It simply has to be seen to be believed; it does not seem possible that anyone could carry such loads which must weigh anything up to one hundred and fifty kilograms.

At number 135 on the left, is the 'Hotel Oriental Home' which in its heyday must have been a very grand establishment indeed (despite the 'Home' in its title). Now sadly dilapidated, you need a little imagination to visualise how it must once have been. Opposite this Hotel is the old City Telegraph and Commercial College which has been operating on this site since 1903.

Once you are past the pavement hawkers, the Street calms down considerably, giving way to the beginning of the gold and jewellery dealers' premises for which this area is well known.

When you reach the next main junction, turn right into Amherst Street where a ten minute walk northwards returns you to the start point.

Chapter 20

Bow Bazar (North)

This jaunt takes in the labyrinth of twisting lanes north of BB Ganguly Street and contained by Amherst Street to the east and College Street to the west.

The starting point is the south eastern corner of the junction of College Street and Surya Sen Street. From here walk southwards along College Street, past the numerous pharmacists, surgical appliances and medical supplies outlets. When you reach number 34, look for a side lane to your left, the entrance is set between two pharmacists' shops. This is Surendra Lal Pyne Lane; narrow and running relatively straight for most of its length. There is not much room in the Lane so it is necessary to keep well over to one side so as to allow the hand pulled rickshaws and other traffic pass through.

At the 'Tut Tuki Hair Cutting Salon', keep over to the right, passing two orange painted buildings, either side of the Lane. At the top of the Lane with the 'Chamber of Astrology' facing you, follow the carriageway as it twists first left then right into Madhu Gupta Lane, shown by one of the old fashioned cast iron street nameplates over to the left.

Continue eastwards along Madhu Gupta Lane, crossing the junction with the wonderfully named, Harish Skidar Path. You will pass by a Doctor's Clinic and one of the ubiquitous Ration Shops to the right. There will very likely be groups of locals standing gossiping outside these places and on corners. Do not be surprised if you are asked if you are lost or need help; so rare is it that westerners are sighted wandering about these parts. You may also be met with looks of incredulity when you explain your reason for being in their neighbourhood voluntarily.

Look out carefully for the next opening on the right; it is narrow, discrete and easy to miss. It is located just past the Government Regulated Oil Shop at number 2A. This is Champatala 1st Bye Lane, a claustrophobically narrow, twisting footpath lined with tiny and tightly packed old houses. Because of the Bye Lane's extreme narrowness (hardly more than one metre at best) and its half quadrant curve to the right, you will have no view of the end until you are almost on top of it. Imagine yourself walking this after dark! Have confidence and carry on; the Bye Lane really does lead somewhere. You will be even more of a rarity here than you were earlier in Madhu Gupta Lane and may well face a few polite enquiries from residents as to what brings you to their neck of the woods. When I am here, the fact that I will be making notes only adds to the locals' intrigue: many peering into my notebook, it making no more sense to them that it would to me were I looking at Bengali script.

Where the Bye Lane finally emerges almost opposite an insalubrious public urinal, turn right. This is the infamous Prem Chand Borel Street. This first part of the Street, which runs straight for the next one hundred and fifty metres or so, is fairly unremarkable, even quite respectable. There are small workshops, outside of which things are being fashioned in wood, plastic and light sheet metals, often with the aid of those old fashioned pedal operated fretsaws. There is one chap who I have become to be on nodding terms with, who works one of these fretsaws outside his premises. He seems mostly to manufacture shop signs and is amazingly skilful. Best of all is that he never seems to mind you watching him work; it seems to amuse him. This part of the Street is also one of those places you will see the children playing shuttlecock. Some are very adept at it, particularly the girls.

Where the Street turns at ninety degrees to the left, its character changes dramatically. Prem Chand Borel Street is one of Calcutta's oldest and most active red light areas, as will be evident from this point on. There will be scores of extravagantly dressed and painted ladies sitting or standing singly and in groups around the doorways of the crumbling old buildings lining each side of the Street or at the narrow entrances to the tiny side lanes leading off. Amongst these there will be a few males made up and dressed as ladies. I do not believe these are Hijera in the true sense, rather they may be catering for a niche market. There is one in particular to whom I must have become a familiar face since, disquietingly, he often favours me with a smile and a wave. He is remarkably unconvincing in female guise.

A few years back I was with my wife passing through this part of the Street when the Police raided one of the buildings. It was very dramatic; a van screeched to a halt, disgorging about a dozen cops who tore into the building with much banging on doors and raised voices. One immediate effect was that many who had been hanging around in the vicinity of the target property, suddenly vanished like rabbits down a warren; one second they were there, the next not a trace of them. In the end it was all a bit of an anti-climax; nobody was led out of the building in handcuffs, nobody apparently arrested even. After five minutes or so the cops shuffled back out of the building, climbed into their van and departed.

The Street opens out into a small square, well actually more of a triangle. There is a small Hindu Temple to the right and a number of chai stalls over to the left. This area will generally be crowded with ladies; as dusk falls it becomes packed with them. They are lounging outside the buildings, standing about in the street and gossiping. Some will be applying make up to a colleague while others will, disconcertingly, be searching the hair of a fellow worker for nits. For those interested, there is a disreputable little lane which runs right around the back of the Hindu Temple, ending back in the Street. It has what may be called 'atmosphere'.

Close by the Temple, I once witnessed something quite remarkable. Outside one of the crumbling houses of dubious repute, a shambling drunk had plonked himself down by the doorstep. He really was in a disgraceful state, muttering, cursing and dribbling all down his shirt front. The ladies of the house came out shouting at him, threatening physical force if he did not remove himself from their doorstep. Clearly they believed his unseemly presence was giving their patch a bad name and acting as a disincentive to respectable potential clients. The ladies triumphed in shooing him away; he never stood a chance.

What needs to be understood about red light areas such as this is that they are rarely as seedy or intimidating as their counterparts in many western cities. For a start there is much more going on than simply the traditional trade of the red light district. Most such areas in Calcutta are also residential neighbourhoods, with local residents carrying on with their ordinary day lives. There will local children with their satchels and rucksacks walking to and from school; youngsters playing street cricket or shuttlecock, housewives out shopping for vegetables and people coming and going from their places of work. The coexistence of these different activities is quite remarkable. It must also be understood that is these places prostitution is driven mainly by poverty not drug dependency as is so often the case in the west.

BOW BAZAR (NORTH)

That accepted, this and other areas like Sonagachi, whilst perfectly safe to navigate during daylight hours are not recommended once night has fallen. Here particularly, with its maze of narrow lanes, it is very easy to get lost after dark unless you really know your way about; knowing which lane leads where and what are the quickest routes out onto the main thoroughfares.

As you walk westwards past the Hindu Temple, the Street narrows and straightens out. Lined with dilapidated old buildings whose leprous facades show a patchwork of brick where decayed rendering has flaked off. There are numerous little cubby hole shops, many selling a bewildering variety of goods given their tiny dimensions. There are also a few small bakeries with inviting displays of the various sweet concoctions so beloved of Bengalis. To both the left and the right are the entrances to tiny interconnecting by lanes in many of which, red light activity is prevalent.

Immediately opposite number 88 and next to a small blue painted Hindu shrine, turn left into Nabin Chandra Borel Lane. This Lane, the erstwhile Harkutta Gullee, was at one time a byword for iniquity; possibly the most notorious part of an already notorious neighbourhood. This serpentine Lane twists first to the left then right before emerging into BB Ganguly Street opposite the 'Tiny Tots Nursery School'. Walk along the Lane using the left hand pavement and return on the right, even if only to be able to say you have done so. Today it is a fairly respectable place, at least in daylight hours.

Returning to Prem Chand Borel Street, turn left and continue westwards. I was passing along this stretch one afternoon when a dishevelled looking lady who had been seated on a plastic stool, suddenly fell forward right in my path, striking her head quite badly it seemed on the pavement. Fearing she had been badly hurt by the impact, I attempted to raise her to administer any necessary first aid. Local bystanders made no attempt at all to assist and seemed completely disinterested in the lady's plight. When in some exasperation I asked them why they would not help, I was told calmly that this was an everyday occurrence; the victim being a notorious habitual drunkard. By the time I had cleaned up the nasty graze on the lady' forehead and applied an Elastoplast, two of her drinking companions had turned up and I was glad to leave the lady in their care.

One spin off from this was an invitation by one of the onlookers to have a look at the tenement in which he lived and those adjoining. As was found in Sett Bagan Gullee at Chapter 11, a single small entrance door off the Street would lead through to a maze of corridors, landings and half landings connected by a system of damp and crumbling brick stairways leading this way and that. You had the distinct impression that, saving for breaks in the building line to accommodate the various lanes, you could travel from tenement to tenement from one end of the Street to the other, without ever setting foot in the carriageway. One such tenement even had its own Kali Shrine, much in use by the residents.

Passing to your right the junction with Gobinda Sen Lane, take the next turning on your right (in fact the last turning in the Street), into Madan Gopal Lane. This narrow and congested Lane contains many ancient domestic buildings, of mainly two and three storeys. The Lane performs a kind of chicane about midpoint then straightens out for the last fifty metres or so before ending at College Street. Turn right out of the Lane and the start point lies a few minutes' walk northwards.

Chapter 21

BOW BAZAR (SOUTH)

This little outing covers the area south of BB Ganguly Street between Sashi Bhusan Dey Street to the east and College Street/Nirmal Chandra Street to the west.

The starting point is the north western corner of the junction of BB Ganguly Street with Amherst Street, opposite the Bank of India branch and diagonal to the forbidding Hotel Kolkata.

This section of BB Ganguly Street, down to the junction with College Street, is noted for its gold and jewellery outlets. It is not only sales which take place here but manufacture as well. Behind the shop premises and tucked away down the many tiny side lanes are numerous small workshops turning out masterpieces in precious metals.

Begin by turning right into BB Ganguly Street, keeping over to the right hand pavement. Some of the jewellery shops you pass are quite small, others large and opulent with armed security guards manning the doors.

Wander as far down the Street as you want then cross over and return along the opposite pavement. In many of the narrow lanes branching off each side of the Street, there is another, clandestine industry which takes place during the early hours of the morning. It is something I have witnessed myself a number of times. This is the painstaking work of gold scavenging, so far as I know unique in Calcutta, being confined to this small area. The process begins after dark when the main roads are empty and the side lanes deserted. Groups of men appear and lift the manholes and inspection covers to the drains. One man, standing or crouching in the drain, digs out the silt and slurry which is then carefully sieved by his colleagues. The object is to extract any residue and miniscule particles of gold flushed into the system from nearby jewellery workshops. The pickings are small, perhaps a quarter the size of a postage stamp would be considered a good return for a whole night's labour.

Leaving BB Ganguly Street, turn right into Ram Kanai Adhikari Lane. This is the sixth turning on the right from the College Street junction and the first on the left from the Amherst Street junction. This Lane and other nearby lanes and by lanes, date back to the latter part of the eighteenth century and contain some of the oldest residential buildings to be found anywhere in Calcutta. This historic Lane was once known as St James' Lane and long before that as Scavengers' Lane.

At the first of the many bends in Ram Kanai Adhikari Lane is a set of public standpipes usually thronged with local housewives, laundering clothes and exchanging neighbourhood tittle-tattle. They are momentarily hushed as I stroll by; some are watchful of this interloping firanghee, others smile shyly. Ten metres past and the chatter resumes as before. There are some tiny unnamed gullees leading off to both left and right, barely more than footpath width. Those off to the right are also, so far as I can ascertain, also unmapped. The Lane comes to an end where it meets Sil Lane which, confusingly, is also known as Babu Ram Seal Lane.

BOW BAZAR (SOUTH)

Turning left into Sil Lane, over to the left is a huge decaying old mansion. The narrowness of the Lane at this point makes is very difficult to take in the detail of the upper storeys; you would need a decent sized ladder to do that. Nearby is the Jumuna Bhavan, painted in singular fashion in a mix of orange, purple and green. About fifty metres on, turn right into an unsigned narrow gullee which leads through to Hideram Banerji Lane.

Hideram Banerji Lane runs parallel to BB Ganguly Street. The Lane begins at Sashi Bhusan Dey Street, twenty metres east and curves gracefully westwards all the way to College Street at the point where the latter becomes Nirmal Chandra Street. The Lane contains many late eighteenth and early nineteenth century residential buildings, some of which are prime for listing as having heritage status. Turning into the Lane, I see a group of Hijeras congregating outside one of the houses; a sure sign that there is either a wedding party or baby naming ceremony going on. For the Hijeras such events provide a lucrative opportunity for them to gather and make such a spectacle and nuisance of themselves that they are paid to go away.

Hijeras are the eunuchs who live on the fringes of Indian society. The term hijera covers those who are biologically male or intersex and have been castrated early in life with all the hormonal consequences that involves, or they have been designated male at birth but adopt feminine gender identity roles and wear women's clothes. They suffer huge discrimination in almost every sphere of life and it is unsurprising therefore that they have created their own society with a sophisticated hierarchical structure. They have even developed their own language called 'Gupti'.

Walking westwards along the Lane, to your left opposite number 51 is Panchanantala Lane. As you enter this Lane there is a small Hindu Temple to your left. The Lane has an important historical connection being where the nineteenth century social reformer and educationalist, Ishwardchandra Vidyasasgar (1820-1891), lived when he first came to Calcutta.

As you progress southwards, the Lane narrows somewhat and to the left leads through to a number of tiny by lanes. The neighbourhood, being primarily residential in character, attracts a lot of hawkers of the peripatetic variety; wandering from lane to lane proclaiming loudly whatever they have to offer. There will be the doodh walla, the chap who sells milk door to door. Others will hawk bread or vegetables and all manner of other domestic necessities. You may even bump into the twig broom seller or his brother in trade, the wonderful ful jharu walla. He is the chap who hawks those long bamboo poles with a kind of feather duster attached to one end; just the sort of implement of use in removing cobwebs and so on, from those hard to reach places. 'Ful Jharu Bikri Hobe' he cries (selling ful jharu), as he wanders about; his stock of unlikely domestic aids balanced on his shoulder.

The Lane curves sharply to the right and becomes Mullick's Dispensary Lane although no trace of this or any other dispensary survives. Take the first turning on the right into Dhiren Dhar Sarani and twenty metres on turn right again into Govinda Sarkar Lane. This Lane also contains some very old buildings, some of them in pretty poor condition. Narrow side lanes branch off to the left forming a labyrinth of interconnecting access ways.

The Lane bends sharply to the right then straightens out for the last fifty metres before it joins Hideram Banerji Lane.

Turn left into Hideram Banerji Lane and continue westwards. The old buildings lining both sides of the Lane are in varying stages of decay; some being downright decrepit. None could be said to be reasonably maintained externally. It has always struck me as odd why so little attention seems to be given to maintaining buildings. You could reasonably say this of India generally but it is particularly apparent in Calcutta which has so many fine buildings at risk by reason of neglect not to mention predatory developers. It is almost as if from the day a building was completed, nobody thereafter ever thought of the need for preventative maintenance, even simple periodic repainting. The result is everywhere to be seen; woodwork rotting and bleached grey by the elements, faded leprous frontages erupting in patches of flaking paint and blown plaster.

When you come to number 3B 'Puja Enterprises', next door to the 'Central Physiotherapy Clinic', turn right into Gaur Dey Lane. This short Lane becomes progressively narrower, accentuated by the height of the buildings lining either side. By the time the Lane ends at BB Ganguly Street is barely two metres in width.

On arriving at BB Ganguly Street, turn left and the junction with College Street/Nirmal Chandra Street is less than a two minute walk. From there to return to the start point, turn right and the junction with Amherst Street is a ten minute walk away.

Chapter 22

Raja Bazar (North)

As with many of the other neighbourhoods explored in this book, my Bengali friend Udita throws up her hands in despair when I tell her I plan to wander around Raja Bazar. 'It is not a good place.' She says 'but if you are determined to go, then be careful.'

Raja Bazar or at least a small part of it, has that reputation. Why? I don't know but it has. It may be because areas like Raja Bazar, Rambagan, and Tiretta and so on, are only infrequently visited by Calcutta's middle classes but are fixed in their minds as comprising insalubrious and teeming back streets, steeped in dirt, decay and even criminality with rumour and hearsay completing the picture.

The Raja Bazar crossing is the busy junction where Keshab Sen Street crosses Achayra Prafulla Chandra (APC) Road, erstwhile Upper Circular Road. The name Raja Bazar also applies to the area which runs in a strip just west of APC Road from around Mahendra Srimani Street, south to beyond Surya Sen Street, almost to the approaches to the Sealdah Flyover.

A convenient starting point is the north western corner of the junction of Keshab Sen Street with APC Road. The junction

RAJA BAZAR (NORTH)

is frantically busy with pavement traders, occupying almost every square metre; you need to pick your way through them carefully.

Dominating this end of Keshab Sen Street is an enormous Mosque whose noble minarets soar above all nearby buildings. Walk back along Keshab Sen Street in the direction of the Mosque and keep a look out for number 155, the 'Bismillah Tea Centre'. Just here, turn right into Girish Vidya Ratna Lane. A word of caution here. All the maze of interconnecting lanes hereabouts go by this collective name which will not be found on any map; at least none I have seen.

The Lane adequately fulfils every reservation about the area held by my friend Udita and my other Bengali colleagues. It is indescribably congested and equally squalid. The Lane and its offshoots are wreathed in swirling smoke from the charcoal and dung fuelled cooking fires of the numerous outdoor caterers found here; in the absence of any breeze it is so bad that visibility is noticeably reduced. Every square centimetre of the decaying buildings lining the lanes here is given over to small scale industries of every description. There are print shops, paint shops, sandal makers, tinsmiths and light engineering of various types. The noise is deafening, seeming to echo back and forth through the narrow thoroughfares. There are goats, either tethered in groups or roaming around freely and getting in your way. This and the scores of chickens constantly getting under your feet, add to the general chaos of the place.

Raja Bazar is largely a Muslim area, this particular locality being almost exclusively so and almost certainly the poorest. On my last visit whilst researching this book, every part of the Lane and its offshoots had long deep excavations running down the centre; sewer or drainage works I supposed. The soaking foetid soil was piled high on either sides of these trenches making navigation akin to an assault course.

If you take the first turning on your left, then left again, you return to the relative sanity of Keshab Sen Street, opposite the 'Imxam Stores' at number 166. Turning right here, look out for a small Hindu shrine about fifty metres further on. Just before the shrine, turn right into Kalidas Singhee Lane.

This Lane is lined with tiny single storey houses, each no larger than one smallish room. The doors to these simple dwellings will more than likely all be standing open with the inhabitants getting on with their lives out in the Lane. So cramped are these dwelling that in many have been adapted by adding a kind of half floor a metre or so off the ground, providing a sleeping platform and thus freeing up precious floor space. Compared to what has gone before, the Lane is a fairly civilised place in its own way.

The Lane follows a series of twists and turns before it emerges into Biplabi Pulin Das Street. Turn right here and follow the Street down until you come to a large green, three storey corner house. This is Lotus Lodge, a rather grand residential property with intricately ornamented balconies to the two upper storeys. Turning right by the Lodge, you enter Parsi Bagan Street (appearing as 'Parshi Bagan Lane' on the old cast iron street nameplate over to the right). Almost the entire right hand side of the Street is dominated by an enormous blue painted building. This is the College of Science and Technology of the University of Calcutta which fronts onto APC Road.

At the end of the Street, turn left into APC Road and passing by the Basu Biggan Mandir and the Bose Institute, take the next turning on the left into Vidyasagar Street. There are often several cows with calves congregating at this point and you may need to gently shoo them aside to allow you to pass through. I was doing just this when I was approached by a friendly, uniformed lady who I took to be the local postie. She engaged me in a lengthy conversation, conducted entirely in Bengali. My nods and smiles must have been well timed since she favoured me with a lovely smile before bidding me Farwell. Of course I had not understood a single word she had said but nevertheless felt rather pleased to have added favourably to Anglo Bengali relations.

The Street contains some very large three storey residential buildings of mixed architectural merit. Number 4 is very fine even down to its pretty side entrance. The immediately neighbouring properties are less pleasing, having had their best features 'improved' away. The Street is a quiet and pleasant backwater which ends abruptly opposite Hrishikesh Park in Brindaban Mullick Lane.

The Park contains a pumping station one of a series designed to prevent flooding in the area from the heavy monsoon rains. Despite this, there is still regular flooding when the drainage outfall located nearby in APC Road silts up, bringing the pumping station's efforts to naught. When this happens, rowboats in the thoroughfares of the vicinity are a common sight.

Turn left into Brindaban Mullick Lane and head southwards past the numerous rotting and decaying buildings lining both sides of the thoroughfare. Where the Lane meets Panchanan Ghosh Lane, turn sharp left then sharp right into Fakir Chand Mitra Lane. The Lane narrows the further south you proceed. It will be full of people sitting about outside of more tiny, simple single story houses. There are scores of small children about, playing the sort of games played by children everywhere. Here you have become another of their games as they crowd around, each wanting to shake your hand and asking 'how are you?' then answering 'fine thank you.' There is also a lot of laundry to contend with, strung out all across the Lane to dry in the sun. If like me you are fairly tall, navigating your way down the Lane will involve a lot of ducking.

On the right as you near the end of the Lane is a small Hindu Temple. All around this are numerous small workshops, several of which contain small, old fashioned printing presses. One is busy producing the rubber soles for flip flops.

A short way past the Temple, the Lane spills out into Keshab Sen Street. A few minutes' walk to the right brings you to the junction with Amherst Street. A ten minute walk to your right returns you to the start point.

Chapter 23

Raja Bazar (South)

As with the last chapter, the madly busy Keshab Sen Street/ APC Road crossing acts as the starting point, in this case the south western corner of the junction.

This is actually a very popular bathing spot with men soaping themselves whilst grouped around the gushing pavement standpipes. This corner of the junction is every bit as busy and hectic as that already experienced opposite. There are large numbers of pavement hawkers, their wares spread and piled all over the place obstructing your passage.

Picking your way through all this, walk westwards down Keshab Sen Street. This side of the Street affords a better view of the huge Mosque opposite. From here you get a much better idea of just how big it is. There are more beggars than is usual occupying the pavements all along the frontage of the Mosque; taking advantage of Islam's teachings on the giving of alms to the poor.

When you get to number 168D 'Globe Fabrics – Ready Made and Tailoring', turn left into Munchi Nakibulla Lane. This narrow, festering thoroughfare is so crowded there is hardly room to move through. The throng of pedestrians is bad enough but attempting to move through all this disorder are men on bicycles, pulling carts and rickshaws even the odd madman on a clapped out and smoking motorbike, adding to the already heavily polluted atmosphere. The din in the Lane is appalling, everyone having to shout to be heard by their companions above the hubbub. Amazingly, you will see people making and receiving calls on their mobile phones. How they manage this amid the all-pervading cacophony is a mystery to me. Perhaps it is a matter of getting accustomed to it; I am not sure I ever could.

As, with some difficulty, you make your way down the Lane, you pass to either side, dark narrow passageways leading through to the backs of the shops and other premises. To the right, these also lead through to a maze of tiny unnamed gullees which lie just behind the buildings fronting the southern side of Keshab Sen Street. These are well used by those taking short cuts or delivering and collecting goods. It is strictly single file as there is insufficient room to allow two people to pass abreast.

The Lane comes to an end at Patwar Bagan Lane which is one of those thoroughfares which branches off here, there and everywhere. Keep hard over to the right hand side and take the branch which veers off diagonally to the right. Patwar Bagan Lane is every bit as frenetic as what went before. Here the overwhelming trade is stationery in all its forms. Huge stacks of paper, cardboard, notebooks and the like, piled everywhere and being shifted to and fro, almost invariably by manual means alone. There is another Mosque dead ahead, the entrance almost hidden behind tottering piles of goods stacked on the pavement and awaiting collection.

The Lane bends to the right before ending at Kali Shome Street. On entering the Street it is akin to having travelled in a dark tunnel and suddenly emerging into the daylight. An altogether wider, more open thoroughfare which runs from APC Road in the east to Baithakkhana Road to the west. Turning right into the Street, cross to the left hand pavement. When you come to 'The Anglo Adult Night High School', a corner premises, turn left into Budhu Ostager Lane.

Budhu Ostager Lane is packed with more dealers in cardboard and paper in all its various forms and boasts a number of small printing works; ancient presses clattering away, spewing out handbills, posters, flyers and other material.

Take the first significant turning on your left into Anthony Bagan Lane. Although the printing trade continues as you progress down the Lane, this is a much calmer thoroughfare by far, offering a brief respite. You will pass by a Hindu Temple to the right and a little further along at number 13 is a once grand old house with a pleasingly elaborate entranceway.

As you near APC Road, identifiable by the modern high rise development visible in the near distance and just by the green painted entrance doors to 'Universal Traders and Suppliers' at number 6, take the small turning on the right. This is the southern arm of Anthony Bagan Lane, a much narrower thoroughfare altogether. This stretch of the Lane turns left then right before meeting a tee junction where a very narrow gullee crosses. Turn left here, passing a street stand pipe in one of those ancient ornamental iron bollard type housings, complete with lion's head relief. You emerge into APC Road next to the 'Jamuna Pharmacy' at number 42.

If you look to your right along APC Road, you can just make out the beginning of the Sealdah flyover in the distance, beyond the Surya Sen Street junction. Your route lies to the left along APC Road.

APC Road is one of the wider thoroughfares of Calcutta, divided by a central barrier and is normally heavily congested with traffic. It is also a tram route in both directions; the clanking monsters plying between Belgachia and Bidhan Nager south to the central destinations of Esplanade, Dalhousie Square and the Howrah Bridge.

The Road follows the line of the old Maratha Ditch; the ancient line of defence for Calcutta, described earlier in chapter 16.

Walking northwards, you pass by on the left, the Victoria Institution College a noted and highly respected educational establishment for women. Roughly opposite on the far side of the Road is the Raja Bazar Tram Depot; a place of loud clanking, hammering, grinding and other sounds of repair and maintenance. For those interested in taking a closer look the Depot can be accessed by using the pedestrian over bridge which you can see a little further northwards. The alternative involves braving the hurtling traffic then locating and squeezing through any convenient gap in the railings running down the centre of the carriageway, an option favoured only by local risk takers in a particular hurry.

There are a lot of pavement settlements strung out along this stretch of APC Road. Wretched hovels cobbled together with bits of old timber tin and tarpaulin and housing whole families. What a contrast with the high rise luxury apartments within eyesight, just to the east of the Road. I meet a lady here, a Bangladeshi with perfect English, learned she said, in the Catholic school she attended in her hometown near Dhaka. Her husband she explained had injured his foot and was absent seeking treatment at a free clinic. She, her husband (almost certainly in India illegally) and their four year old son lived here under a tarpaulin stretched across the pavement railings. 'What can we do?' she told me, 'we hope for better'. I too share that hope.

A little further on and almost hidden by a petrol station on your left, is the ruin of a once magnificent old mansion. It is in an appalling state of dilapidation and gives every appearance of having been abandoned decades ago. It is popularly believed locally to be haunted which is probably why it has not been squatted by the pavement dwellers hereabouts.

Just past this 'haunted' old mansion, you reach the junction with Keshab Sen Street, the starting point.

Chapter 24

Burra Bazar (North)

Burra Bazar (sometimes termed Bara Bazar), covers an area which lies between Canning Street to the south, Kali Krishna Tagore Street to the north, Rabindra Sarani to the east and the River Hooghly to the west. The entire area is bisected by MG Road which runs centrally, east to west.

The whole market complex which is Burra Bazar is a veritable labyrinth of tiny, winding and interconnecting lanes. It has been described as a world in itself where 'anything and everything is available even tiger's milk if you pay the right price'.

Burra Bazar is divided into a number of sub-markets or 'patties' according to the goods traded. Hence dhotipatti, fancypatti and so on. Further sub-divisions are katra, chowk or kothi although so congested and frenetic is the whole area that it is all but impossible to determine with any accuracy where one sub-division ends and another begins; a subtle change in the type of goods being traded is about the only clue.

Over the years, many of the once large trading outlets have been repeatedly sub-divided into numerous tiny shops or godowns. This, exacerbated by numberless illegal and jerry built extensions or other questionable development, has turned

BURRA BAZAR (NORTH)

many of the Bazar's buildings into seething warrens. You can enter such buildings from one lane, get hopelessly lost in the narrow twisting maze of corridors and stairwells within and emerge a block away in an entirely different lane.

Because of the sheer complexity of the Bazar area, I have divided the exploration of it into two separate routes, north and south to make it more manageable. There is no reason though why the energetic traveller, who can spare the time, cannot combine the two in a single expedition.

To explore the northern route through the Bazar, start from the north western corner of the junction of MG Road with Rabindra Sarani.

MG Road being the principal artery through Burra Bazar and linking Calcutta's two main railway stations, is just about the best place to witness the unbelievable amount of goods which are moved around the City by purely manual means; still the cheapest method of conveyance.

From dawn until well after sunset there is a seemingly endless procession of stupendous loads of every description being carried, pushed or pulled along this congested thoroughfare. You will see the coolie in graceful stride to and from the nearby fruit market balancing on his head a huge box or basket of various fruits or a small haystack of paddy. Another will be going in the opposite direction holding aloft a gigantic netting bundle of brightly coloured plastic pots or buckets. There will almost certainly be one or more delivering large lorry tyres by rolling them along the road, weaving expertly through the heavy traffic. I have seen a single coolie expertly managing three such tyres at a time. You will see teams of anything up to six or eight coolies, some pushing, some pulling, impossibly loaded carts of potatoes, cement, bricks, iron reinforcing rods, almost anything in fact; a virtual lorry load dumped onto a cart. I once stood marvelling at one coolie manoeuvring through the thronged mass of pedestrians and traffic, a five metre ladder, held high above his head, successfully negotiating all of the many obstacles in his path.

Set off westwards down MG Road in the direction of the River and take the fourth turning on the right into Mullick Lane (not to be confused with Mullick Street, which is the more prominent turning before this). Going north, Mullick Lane crosses first Cotton Street then Burtollah (Bartala) Street; two significant thoroughfares of the Bazar which are covered separately in the southern route detailed in the next chapter. The Lane is every bit as busy as MG Road but this bustle is concentrated and confined within a very much narrower space. Trucks, cars, motorcycles, carts, rickshaws and every other form of conveyance will be vying with the multitude of pedestrians for a route through the melee; all this to the cacophony of hooting vehicle horns, the frantic ringing of bicycle bells and the barking of alarmed street dogs.

After passing the junction with Burtollah Street, there are a number of even narrower and more congested lanes to both left and right. Some of these lanes, being so narrow and buildings so high, that they receive little natural daylight at ground level.

At the next main junction, that with Hari Ram Goenka Street, turn to the left. This western arm of the Street, leading down towards the River is packed full of trading outlets and pavement enterprises. Traffic can be very heavy here forcing you out of the roadway and right over against the shop fronts.

Close to the end of Hari Ram Goenka Street, turn right into Nalini Sett (Seth) Road. This is an altogether wider, more open thoroughfare and contains a number of the larger trading houses and godowns. There will be lines of lorries parked outside these premises, in the process of being loaded or unloaded, all by manual means of course.

BURRA BAZAR (NORTH)

Towards the top of the Road and over to the left, is a dismal collection of wretched pavement shanties. Outside these hovels, the inhabitants will be sorting through the fruit of their scavenging forays, separating it into different piles. Others will be soaping themselves at a standpipe while the women will be violently thrashing the laundry against the paving slabs.

Where Nalini Sett Road gives out into a five way junction, turn sharp right into Sovaram Basak Street, a narrow and lively thoroughfare where there is invariably something of interest going on.

Where the Street meets Kalkar Street, the next main junction, cross straight over into Debendra Dutta Lane. This very short Lane ends at Sibtala Street. Turn right here and take the first turning on the left into Shiv Thakur Lane. This narrow twisting Lane is far more residential in character and being relatively free of traffic, provides welcome respite. Both sides of the Lane are lined with ancient and crumbling residential buildings, some very decrepit. About half way down this Lane, at the junction with an unsigned by lane to your left, is a horribly dilapidated building. The four storeys above ground level are seemingly held up by a few decaying brick and concrete columns and just three slim iron supports. Hurry on past; preferably on tip toe.

Just where the Lane performs a left/right chicane, take the narrow turning on the right into the grandly named Sukh Lal Jahuri Lane. This short thoroughfare meets Hari Ram Goenka Street in less than one hundred metres. Turn right into the Street, which is the eastern arm of that visited earlier.

In full swing, Hari Ram Goenka Street can become madly congested with traders and their customers and every type of wheeled traffic. There is something her for everyone. Look to your left for the 'Riddhi Siddhi – House of all Kinds of Bed

Sheet'. A little way past this emporium and to the right is the shop sign for the 'Mona Lisa Ladies Beauty Parlour' which promises 'Gun Shot for Nose and Ears'. Well I know what they mean or at least I hope I do.

A little further along, near 'Sahib Tailoring' is a large sari emporium, usually thronged with elegantly clad ladies assisting relatives in the choice of wedding outfits.

When you reach the junction with Jagmohan Mullick Lane, (the second significant junction), turn left and retrace your earlier steps, crossing first Burtollah Street then Cotton Street. Once you come to Cotton Street, cross straight over into Hanumanji Lane. Here, to your left, is the magnificent, white fronted Jain Temple; an architectural gem.

Follow Hanumanji Lane down its twisting length until it ends at MG Road. Turn left and the start point lies a few minutes' walk eastwards.

Chapter 25

Burra Bazar (South)

This chapter follows a route just to the south of that set out for the first excursion into Burra Bazar in chapter 24.

Using the same starting point, the north western corner of the junction of Rabindra Sarani and MG Road, provides the opportunity to experience further the hectic activity taking place nearby; always rewarding.

Walking westwards along MG Road in the direction of the River, concentrate on the pavement enterprises lining both sides of the thoroughfare.

Opposite the starting point and near the south east corner of the junction is located a very interesting and unusual enterprise. Here, out on the pavement there is a chap who manufactures the charcoal burning braziers one sees in use at almost every pavement food stall. The process begins with an open topped round tin container, about one fifth the size of the conventional oil drum. This is lined with a layer of wet clay about five centimetres thick. These are then lined up along the pavement so that the clay can dry in the sun. A series of holes are then made in each side of the clay lined drum about half way up. Thin metal rods are then passed through to form a platform.

On this platform, charcoal is placed and burned, baking the clay rock hard. The brazier is then ready for the use intended. Usually there are anything up to thirty of these devices, at various stages of construction, lined up all along the pavement.

Close to this enterprise, used to be the regular pitch of a lady I came to name to myself as Enigma. Judging by her hair and features she could well have been a tribal from the hinterlands of Bengal and how she came to be there on the streets of Calcutta was anyone's guess. She could have been any age from thirty to sixty; never looking any different in all the years I was aware of her. I never saw her beg or even talk to anyone. She would arrive after sunrise and depart just before sunset; no one seemed to know any more than that about her. A few visits back, she had vanished and I have not seen her since.

Over on the left hand pavement are the massed stalls of traders in all kinds of clothing and textiles. What they stock never seems to change regardless of the season and prevailing climate. I have passed by when temperatures have been hovering around 40 degrees centigrade with stalls piled high with heavy blankets, thick woolly jumpers and monkey hats complete with thermal padded ear flaps. Conversely, in January when temperatures are down to 10 degrees centigrade, (positively freezing for most locals), flip flops, shorts and singlets are being offered in abundance. There will be those trading in nothing but those 'party dresses', favoured all over India for clothing young daughters; often quite fantastic creations, thick with chiffon, flounces, puffed shoulders, sequins and silk ribbons. As pretty as they are impractical.

Back over on the right hand pavement, outside of the textile dealers, sit men at those antique treadle sewing machines, turning out all sorts of garments. There will be the occasional letter writer clacking away on their ancient manual typewriter, most likely positioned near to the Burra Bazar Post Office.

BURRA BAZAR (SOUTH)

There will be a whole range of pavement catering operations being conducted from large containers of sizzling, smoking oil; perfectly round small dosas being produced in double quick time then neatly piled for sale to the passing peckish.

There are also any number of pavement cobblers in evidence along this stretch of the pavement. With their box of tools and old fashioned iron shoe last they offer everything from fixing a loose sandal buckle or strap to complete resoling. Many will also repair or refurbish your umbrella, replacing snapped struts or patching the fabric.

One particular pavement enterprise is worth special mention. This is involved in the repair of bags and cases, anything from handbags and attaché cases to large suitcases and trunks. They have boxes and boxes of catches, buckles, straps, handles and locks of every description and appear to do a roaring trade.

When you reach the junction with Basanta Lal Muraka Street, turn right. Follow the Street the short distance until it meets Cotton Street, in reality not much more than a lane at this point. Turn left into Cotton Street then take the first turning on the right into the southern end of Nalini Sett Road. This part of the Road is home to many a bullion dealer and gold and silver refiners; hard to reconcile with the humble shop fronts proclaiming this.

At the next junction, with Burtollah Street leading off the right, take a short diversion by turning left into Mirbahar Ghat Street. A short way down the Street provides an unusual end on view of the great Howrah Bridge; not often seen from this angle.

Retrace your steps to the junction then cross straight over into Burtollah Street, a hugely busy artery through this southern section of Burra Bazar. The Street is quite difficult to negotiate because of the lawless traffic using it as a cut through from

Strand Road to Rabindra Sarani. This is made worse by the equally lawless traffic emerging from and entering the numerous side lanes to both left and right.

Horrendously jerry built extensions to buildings and other illegal over development of sites, is endemic throughout Burra Bazar and this particular location provides many prime examples. Civic records suggest that as many as eighty percent of the buildings in Burra Bazar are illegal in the sense that they have been built, extended or otherwise altered without any planning or building consents. This is exacerbated by the scant regard given to structural integrity or access arrangements in the already severely congested and narrow lanes which make up much of the area.

The Calcutta Municipal Corporation has estimated that around 600 buildings in Burra Bazar can be classed as hazardous and a further 500 classed as medium to high risk. Anyone who has explored Burra Bazar for themselves could be forgiven for thinking even these alarming figures to be actually on the conservative side. The West Bengal Fire and Rescue Service cite the total collapse of 5 buildings in Burra Bazar and the partial collapse of 30 others in 2007 alone. In all of these buildings it was reported that anything up to 100 tiny shops had been built on each floor by erecting plywood partitions. Risk of structural collapse aside, the potential fire hazard posed by this is doubly alarming.

Once you reach the junction with Jagmohan Mullick Lane, turn left and cross to the right hand pavement. Here you can see some extremely artistic displays of fruit and vegetables on the stalls of the pavement traders; those of the beautifully presented red and green chillies are particularly attractive.

Take the next turning on the right into Madho Kristo Seth Lane, marked by the well patronised 'Bapu Tea Stall' on

BURRA BAZAR (SOUTH)

the corner together with a Police Post taking up at least half the width of the Lane. At the next junction cross straight over into Hanspukar 1st Lane. This narrow little thoroughfare is usually wreathed in smoke from the cooking fires of the numerous pavement food stalls operating here. The Lane is lined with crumbling old three and four storey buildings which accentuates the narrowness.

The Lane winds on until at no obviously definable point it morphs into Kanulal Lane. It may be that this name change occurs just where a crazily located and quite likely illegal, building forces you into a tiny passageway past it, to the right.

Kanulal Lane is a short thoroughfare, dominated by an ancient old building to one side, the top three storeys of which project out over the Lane below to an alarming degree.

At the end of Kanulal Lane by 'Discount Optics', turn right into Adi Banstalla Lane, then right again into the eastern end of Burtollah Street. The Street is one of the main east/west arteries through the Bazar but despite this. Is unnervingly narrow. There is much leaping aside to avoid the oncoming carts, rickshaws, motorcycles and other vehicles. At the same time it is necessary to keep a look out to either side and to the rear to spot what may be sneaking up on you. Quite apart from having to negotiate through all this, there will be further obstacles to contend with in the form of piles of goods piled higgledy piggledy all over the thoroughfare. Crates, boxes and sacks being moved into and out of the retail and wholesale premises lining both sides of the Street and the darkened little by lanes leading off from it.

By the time you reach the major junction with Jagmohan Mullick Lane, you have the feeling of having just come through a kind of urban survival course which has sorely tested all your senses. As busy as this junction is, it is a relief to what you have just come through.

Turning left, you quickly meet Cotton Street (or Utkalmoni Gopabandhu Sarani to give it its official new name – we will stick with Cotton Street). Turn left into the Street which, as its (old) name implies, is packed with tailoring and textile enterprises; the clatter of sewing machines clearly discernable above the general Street hubbub. Almost as congested as Burtollah Street, Cotton Street is plagued with traffic, forcing you right over against the shop fronts at some points. As with much of the Bazar area, the tightly packed and crumbling buildings hereabouts, have been much altered internally by being subdivided into hosts of tiny shops and workshops. I have already referred to the fire risk from such alterations, the extension of that is to imagine the sheer difficulties involved in getting any meaningful firefighting equipment to the scene of any conflagration through the area's narrow, congested lanes.

Very bad fires have occurred in the Bazar, notably the Nandaram Market just south of MG Road. Some five years ago Nandaram was ravaged by a huge fire which destroyed more than 1.200 business and raged for more than forty hours but mercifully, without any loss of life.

As you walk further eastwards along the Street, you pass 'Balaji Tower' on the right; a huge glass fronted building, completely incongruous in the street scene.

Nearing the end of Burtollah Street where it meets Rabindra Sarani, take the last turning on the right into Babulal Lane. The Lane, narrow, dark and wreathed in smoke from cooking fires, rings with the clang of metal pots being scoured in the gutter running along the right hand side. Barely two metres wide, the Lane at ground level, is lined either side by small, cubby hole type tailoring outlets. Little natural daylight reaches ground level in the Lane because of the ramshackle four and even five storey buildings looming over it to either side.

Babulal Lane leads out into MG Road very close to the start point which lies less than one hundred metres to your left.

Chapter 26

THE HOWRAH BRIDGE AND HOWRAH STATION

No trip to Calcutta can be complete without a crossing of the iconic Howrah Bridge to Howrah Station, the great rail terminus on the west bank of the River Hooghly; one of the largest railway complexes in India and among the busiest.

Currently, the nearest Metro station to the Howrah Bridge is MG Road, involving a good twenty minute walk westwards down MG Road from the CR Avenue crossing. The next phase of the Metro extension will provide and east/west line, dipping under the River and providing a stop at Howrah Station but that will not become a reality for a number of years. For those unwilling to brave MG Road on foot, trams numbers 11, 15/12, 20, 21 and 26 run from the MG Road/CR Avenue junction and terminate at the eastern side of the Howrah Bridge.

Whatever way you arrive, your approach to the Bridge will be via the gradual incline rising from Strand Road. At any time this will be teeming with a mass of people approaching and leaving what is one of the busiest bridges on earth; the massive and iconic Howrah Bridge. The Bridge was officially renamed

Rabindra Setu in 1965, in honour of India's first Nobel Laureate, Rabindranath Tagore.

The Bridge which links Howrah on the west bank of the River Hooghly with Calcutta proper on the east bank was constructed between 1937 and 1943. It replaced a floating pontoon type bridge built in 1874 by Sir Bradford Leslie. This earlier bridge had hinged shore spans to accommodate the Hooghly's tides. At the highest tides, these hinged spans became so steep that the bullock carts (which as late as 1910 still made up more than half of all vehicular traffic), were unable to negotiate passage. The old bridge could be opened to allow the passage of River traffic but was clearly inadequate to cope with the ever increasing traffic between Howrah and Calcutta.

Recognition of the need for a new bridge to span the Hooghly, stretched back to the early years of the twentieth century but more than three decades of indecision by the Government of Bengal were to pass before the designs of consultant engineers, Rendell, Palmer and Tritton, for a replacement bridge was accepted. All this delay was a regular source of barbed and amusing contributions to the letters columns of Calcutta's Statesman newspaper and the Municipal Gazette. One wag, an anonymous Englishman signing himself 'Diogenes' even submitted a satirical poem lampooning it all.

The new Bridge was to be of the suspension type, balanced cantilever pattern. It was constructed by Cleveland Bridge and Engineering Co Ltd of Darlington, England. A total of 26,500 tons of steel were used in the construction, nearly all of which was supplied by the Indian firm of Tata Iron and Steel Co. Fabrication of the steel was undertaken by Braithwaite, Burn and Jessop Co. at several different locations throughout Calcutta. Interestingly, the cast iron nameplate of the original Jessop Engineers can still be found affixed to structures all over the City, notably at several of the ferry ghats along the River.

THE HOWRAH BRIDGE AND HOWRAH STATION

The Bridge is approximately seven hundred metres long and thirty metres wide with the two main supporting towers rising to almost ninety metres. It is said that on hot days the Bridge expands by as much as ten centimetres.

The level of traffic carried by the Bridge is phenomenal. Recent census surveys give a daily figure of 150,000 vehicles of all descriptions and a staggering 3 million pedestrian movements. Up to the early 1990's the road deck of the Bridge also carried trams in both directions, to and from Howrah Station. At one time congestion on the Bridge was very much worse than it is today, when before the building of the Vidyasagar Bridge downstream and the Vivekananda Bridge upstream, this was the only fixed crossing.

Maintenance of the Bridge is almost perpetual; there always seem to be something going on. There have been very few occasions when I have crossed without witnessing the amazing balancing feats of maintenance workers perched precariously high above, amidst the maze of iron girders. One fairly recent maintenance item has been the fitting of protective covers to the bases of the stanchions rising from the road deck. Alarm bells had rung when it was found that the constant coating with red spit from Paan users was causing serious corrosion. The protective covers have not stopped the spitting but have at least provided a barrier to its deleterious effects. As I write, the Bridge is undergoing its first complete repaint in eight years; a monumental task which will devour an astonishing 26,000 litres of paint.

There is a generous footpath provided either side of the road deck of which almost every square metre will be in use from sunrise to well after sunset. Cross on one footpath and return on the other. On the outward leg, stick to the southern (left) footpath, from where, looking over the parapet, you can see the Mullick Ghat Flower Market. The wonderful riot of colours the Market provides is stunning, particularly when viewed from the Bridge. Next to the Market is the Armenian Ghat where muscled fitness enthusiasts can be seen going through their exercise routines.

Whatever can be carried or carted and much that seems improbable, is ferried back and forth across the Bridge in a seemingly endless procession between the markets of Burra Bazar and the railway stations and godowns of Sealdah and Howrah. Some of the loads being shifted are awe inspiring; great bundles stitched up in calico or contained in netting balanced on the heads of coolies as they move at a surprising pace along the thronged walkways. If you are lucky you may see the occasional coolie expertly rolling along a kind of giant hoop, taller than himself, made up of coiled piping or cable. On the road deck itself you will find teams of coolies, four or six strong, pulling and pushing impossibly loaded carts back and forth. This is still the most economical way to move goods around a City where labour is cheap, plentiful and expendable.

At either end of the Bridge, but particularly the Howrah end, look out for the skilful exponents of the ancient and ingenious art of 'Kili Josiyam' or fortune telling with parrots. How this practice came about or who thought up this wonderful exhibition is unknown. Some say that it originated in the southern State of Tamil Nadu. Whether this is correct or not, I don't know but I have seen it practised in most parts of India. It works like this. The artiste (for no other term does his performance full justice), sits there on the pavement with his caged small green parrot and his pack of fortune telling cards. Those requiring a consultation squat down beside him whereupon the parrot is summoned from its cage. The parrot is then told your name and often also your birth date and star sign. The parrot then proceeds, using its beak, to flip over, one at a time, cards from the deck. When the parrot finds a card it considers appropriate, it carries it in its beak and hands it over to its master and co-conspirator. That card is then interpreted for you; it contains your fortune and fate which, in essence is all down to the given mood of the parrot. There are a number of possible variations. Some practitioners of the art train their parrots to walk once around its cage each time a card is flipped over; some parrots seem to flip over almost the entire pack before selecting a card, no doubt for dramatic effect. It is an altogether enjoyable and uplifting experience which should not be missed.

Ahead and just to the left of the Bridge is the huge bulk of Howrah Railway Station. From a distance, this great red brick structure could quite easily be mistaken for some great palace or monumental fortification. Indeed this latter possibility is not so far off the mark since the British tended to build Indian railway stations with at least one eye on their ease of defence, should the need arise.

For reasons which will be incomprehensible to the western traveller, you are forbidden to photograph the Howrah Bridge, or indeed anything else from it. To be fair, much the same prohibition applies to every other government structure or building throughout India, from the ultra-sensitive to the entirely mundane. No doubt some dispensation must have been given for the numerous picture postcards of the Bridge widely available from most City bookstores.

By far the best view of the Bridge is from the River, mid-stream. Regular ferries operate from the ferry ghat on the Howrah side; more on which later.

On reaching the Howrah side of the Bridge keep over to the left, picking your way through the mass of pavement hawkers and past the foetid, stinking trench to the side of the access road. Keeping the main Station building to your right you pass the bathing ghat to your left followed by the Howrah Ferry Ghat. There is a sort of booking hall where you buy your tickets from barred cubby holes, manned by formidable Bengali matrons. Make sure you go to the right cubby hole; the various destinations being indicated in faded lettering above each respective counter. A one way ticket to, say, Baghbazar, will cost you six and a half rupees. Hang on to your ticket as you may be asked to produce it en route and certainly when docking at your destination.

The main entrance to the Railway Station is almost directly opposite the Ferry Ghat. Just look for the point in the Station frontage where the largest number of people are flowing in and out.

The first rail line from Calcutta was laid in 1854, running here from Howrah northwest to the coalfields of the Bardhaman district of Bengal. This was only the second line in the whole sub-continent, the first being laid a year earlier from Bombay (Mumbai) to Thaney.

The original Howrah Station was little more than a wooden shed adjoining a number of godowns. This was replaced after a few years by a colonnaded building which remained in use right up to the early years of the twentieth century. The present main Station building was completed in 1905 to a design by the British railway engineer, Halsey Ricardo. In the 1980's the Station was extended with a new complex just south of the main building.

Trains from Howrah serve the greater Calcutta urban area, the whole of West Bengal State and most major cities in India. A numbers of India's most important trunk rail routes end at Howrah. The Station handles more than four hundred train movements every day. Upwards of two and a half million people are estimated to pass through the Station daily.

THE HOWRAH BRIDGE AND HOWRAH STATION

Major railway termini the world over, being hubs of human transit are inevitably crowded and busy places. At Howrah this is on a scale which almost beggars belief. Once inside the Station it seems as if half of the population of Calcutta has arrived before you and are either boarding or waiting for outgoing trains, whilst the other half is streaming off arriving trains. To get some idea of the scale of human movement taking place, you need to find some vantage point from where you are within sight of the platform barriers but not in danger of being submerged under the tide of humanity swirling everywhere about you. Once an incoming train grinds metallically to a halt and often before that, doors are flung open and the platform is instantly swamped with alighting passengers. Pressing forward in a seemingly never ending stream, they flow through the barriers, out into the concourse and through the pedestrian underpass and exits, being met by equal numbers coming the other way.

Amidst this contraflow of humanity, there are sitting or laying all over the station concourse, hundreds of waiting passengers, singly or in whole family groups together with their bundles of possessions. Some will be sleeping, some gossiping or eating while others just waiting with that fatalistic patience rarely witnessed outside of India.

Weaving amongst all this chaos are the knowledgeable and indispensable Station coolies with their brass licence badges and red, green or orange work shirts. One look at your ticket and they are off with your luggage held aloft, expertly guiding you through the throng, to the correct platform, the right train and even the right carriage.

The chorus of coolies, hawkers and passengers, of trains pulling in and out, of tinny garbled announcements through battered loudspeakers, all contribute to the general level of mixed din within the Station. Nobody talks at Howrah, everyone shouts; they must if they are to be heard by their neighbour.

On almost any day you can see people from all over the sub-continent passing through the Station. Malayalees and Tamils from the deep south en route to or from Madras, Maduri Trivandrum and Cochin: those from north eastern States like Assam, Meghalaya, Manipur and Tripura; Biharis and Oriyas from neighbouring States and those from further afield, Gujarat, Punjab Maharashtra and Kashmir.

The Station is a kind of township in itself. There are scores of outlets where you can buy anything from fresh fruit, drinks, newspapers and magazines, badges of Hindu deities and every other kind of provision you could possibly need to sustain you on your journey to the other end of India. Here you can have your shoes mended and cleaned, your face shaved, hair cut and your fortune and future told. There is a Mosque, a Temple and even a Railway Court to dispense swift justice to fare dodgers and other miscreants. There was even once a man here who for a small fee, would iron your clothes although I have not seen him operating here for the last few years.

The Station and its environs has almost from the day it was laid out, played host to refugees, the homeless and otherwise rootless and dispossessed. Added to this are the new arrivals to the City, fleeing poverty, debt, their families or the long arm of the law. I can remember in the early 1970's, the large number of refugees camped out here, having fled the conflict in what was to become Bangladesh. By the 1980's there were still scores of these families remaining; still camped out on and around the platforms, almost a decade and a half after the conflict had ended. Some of their children had been born here, never having known any other home.

In recent years by far the largest and most socially disturbing group of Station denizens are the tribes of semi feral children who wind up here from Calcutta's streets, the rural hinterland of Bengal and locations far beyond; forming themselves into tight knit clans for mutual protection and survival.

The Railway Protection Force (RPF) estimate that the whole Station complex, including the goods yards and train sheds, provide shelter for up to three thousands of these children. Living between and beneath the platforms, along the tracks and in the numerous sidings and decaying goods wagons, their presence has become a permanent feature of the place. The overwhelming majority are boys but there are increasing numbers of girls featuring in these clans. Some will have gravitated to Howrah following an earlier career of joyriding India's vast rail network; many being amazingly well travelled. Others have been abandoned, lost or have fled violent or otherwise abusive families. A percentage will have drifted here after having escaped abduction and trafficking.

These children live on their wits and from scavenging and pilfering in and around the Station and on incoming trains. Even before an incoming train has come to a complete stop, gangs of these children will descend like a biblical plague of locusts, carrying off anything discarded by passengers; plastic water bottles, newspapers and half eaten food. They will also carry off anything the unwary or distracted passenger has not kept a very firm hold upon; wallets, purses, handbags, briefcases or cell phones; anything which can be sold or traded is at risk. The inexperienced western traveller is particularly vulnerable, not least because of their possible unwillingness to recognise the degree of risk posed to their possessions from children of such tender years.

The greater numbers of these children will have some form of dependency. Most of these will be solvent abusers; the nauseating smell of glue being everywhere they congregate, sniffing from rags soaked in the stuff. 'Dendrite' seems to be the solvent of choice.

Some of the older children, by which I mean those above, say, twelve years of age, have other drug dependency problems, including crack and heroin addiction.

This widespread dependency is the means by which many of these children have been ensnared by the 'dadas'; the adult gangster ringleaders. These dadas use the children as thieves or couriers of drugs and other contraband, including firearms. It is by no means unusual to read reports in the 'Metro' pages of the Calcutta Telegraph newspaper, of Police arresting children as young as ten or eleven years old, in possession of several firearms or explosives; apprehended in the course of transporting this for others.

These dadas invariably, do not themselves live within the Station precincts. They live mainly outside the Station complex in the surrounding slums and dubious bars of Howrah, beyond the reach of the Railway Protection Force. Many of these dadas were formerly just like the Station children they control, having risen through the ranks, as it were. Amongst their number are some very unpleasant characters; a proportion very nasty indeed and involved in every sphere of criminality from receiving stolen property to extortion and contract killing. These types feature regularly in the wanted lists published by the Calcutta Police and West Bengal Police (the latter being responsible for the Howrah district). These lists, photos and all, are invariably displayed at every Police Station and make interesting reading.

Whilst there is little apparent sympathy for these children from locals and others regularly using Howrah Station, they are not completely abandoned by society. There are a number of charitable organisations concerned for their welfare. One such is the Society for Educational and Environmental Development (SEED). Originally founded for the development of the slum dwellers of Howrah generally, SEED has for the last decade or more worked with children in the streets and within the Station precincts. The Society runs a drop in centre located just outside the Station and two safe night shelters, one for boys, the other for girls, located nearby. SEED also organises 'platform schools' teaching basic literacy and numeracy skills and engaging with the children.

Other valuable work for the welfare of these children, including help with their addiction issues is carried out by the Calcutta Samaritans and the Children in Need Institute (CINI).

Leaving the Station, there is one other very interesting but curiously unpublicised, feature of the complex to see; the Eastern Railway Museum.

The Museum is located about three hundred metres or so south of the main Station building. To get there, walk past the newer Station extension, the old goods warehouses and the prominent water tower. The Museum lies just beyond this last landmark.

The Museum was opened in 2006 and, in terms of scale, is only the second of its kind in the whole of India, the other being in Delhi. The largely open air Museum is housed in a beautifully maintained and completely litter free, park like setting with lush lawns, exotic shrubbery and even ornamental fountains. It is open every day barring Thursdays, from 1.00pm to 8.00pm. Admission will set you back five rupees and, for a further ten rupees, you can have a ride on the miniature train which runs through the grounds.

The Museum houses examples of old and rare steam, diesel and electric locomotives. There are also fully furnished and fitted out passenger carriages from the days when travel by train could be a very grand affair. There are exhibitions of photographs and prints tracing the history of railway development in eastern India. There are a host of artefacts and models recording the evolution of signalling, communications and track laying. There is also a superb model of the Howrah Station complex and the building within most of this is housed is in the same style and materials as the main Howrah Station building; a nice touch.

I have visited the Museum on numerous occasions over the years and have always been surprised at how few visitors there are, unless that is I have always happened upon a slack time. I have rarely seen more than five or six other visitors present, always all of them Indians. The Museum is a gem of a place and it is a pity it is not more widely publicised and promoted.

To return simply involves retracing your steps back past the water tower, the main Station building and back across the Bridge.

Chapter 27

SOUTH PARK STREET CEMETERY

Nowhere is Calcutta's British past more poignantly evident than the South Park Street Cemetery. This imperial necropolis, the last resting place of many of the earliest British inhabitants of Calcutta, is steeped in historical connection to the early development of a muddy trading outpost into a great City.

Here in shaded groves, amongst sepulchral obelisks, sarcophagi, urns, pyramids, catafalques and other funereal and lichen encrusted monuments, lie many of the once great and good, the civil and military servants of the East India Company, the merchants and the professional classes along with their wives and children.

The South Park Street Cemetery is sited at the south western corner of the junction of Park Street/Rawdon Street and the Lower Circular Road (now AJC Bose Road). This is an approximate twenty minute walk southwards down Park Street from the Metro station of that name.

There was once another smaller, and slightly more recent cemetery located immediately opposite our surviving Cemetery, just off the northern side of Park Street. The site of this is now occupied by the Assembly of God Church, the Mission of Mercy Hospital and the Apeejay School. There is just one reminder of this long obliterated cemetery; a single remaining memorial set just to the right of the side of the Hospital facing Park Street. This single monument is the Robertson memorial bearing the details of six members of that family, one of whom was a onetime Commissioner of the Calcutta Police Force.

The South Park Street Cemetery or the 'Great Cemetery' as it was originally known. Is now administered by the Christian Burial Board of Calcutta. The Cemetery opened on 25th August 1767; the first recorded burial taking place that very day; that of John Wood, a writer (clerk) of the Customs House. His grave has since been obliterated, swept away when the Cemetery was later extended. The oldest still existing grave which bears an inscription, is that of Mrs Sarah Pearson, d. 8th September 1768.

In those early days, the Cemetery was 'far out in the country', occupying marshy, forested terrain amidst patches of jungle. It was approached by a lonely raised causeway or bund, later to become Burial Ground Road and later still, present day Park Street. Most burials took place after dark by lantern light. The exceptions were military funerals, employing 'gun carriages and rolling guns'.

Before entering the Cemetery's main gate, you will see just to the left, a memorial erected by the Anglo Indian Association to Henry Vivian Louis Derozio. He was the young Anglo Indian poet, radical and inspiration behind the Young Bengal Movement of the early years of the nineteenth century, I once met here an Indian gentleman visiting Calcutta from Bangalore who was distressed that the British had blocked his burial within the Cemetery. I could see the reason for his misapprehension since the memorial states 'buried here........' I was able to reassure this chap that 'here' actually meant within the actual Cemetery and not beneath the pavement slabs on which the memorial stands. Derozio's tomb is actually diagonal to that of 'Hindoo Stuart' (of whom more later).

Through the Cemetery's main gate (there is another side entrance in nearby Rawdon Street), you enter a portico which houses the office of the Cemetery Superintendent and the surviving archives, comprising an alphabetical list of surnames, cross referenced to grave numbers. These archives can be made available upon request. You will be asked to sign the visitors' book; this also contains a column to add your comments on the way out. Through the portico is the main pathway into the Cemetery; some of the oldest graves being those closest to the entrance.

What most strikes the first time visitor is the haunting, decaying grandeur of the place; the fantastic architecture of death, celebrated with neoclassical mausoleums, pyramid tombs, columns, arches and domed temple like monuments. All of this executed in monumental scale and inscribed with the once fashionable symbols of mortality; crossed canon, swords, scythes, skulls, hour glasses and such like. Then there is the inescapable sensation of tranquillity. It is difficult to believe that the mayhem which is Calcutta in full swing is going on just outside the high boundary walls. The calm serenity of this tree shaded oasis lends much to the sombre and ghostly atmosphere pervading the whole place. You can easily spend hours here wandering the lonely pathways past the decaying tombs whose inscriptions proclaim in elegant and archaic terms the virtues of the deceased.

Rudyard Kipling, never a fan of Calcutta generally, was equally scathing about the Cemetery. He wrote in his 1888 work, 'City of Dreadful Night', *'The tombs are small houses. It is as though we walked down the streets of a town, so tall are they and so closely do they stand – a town shrivelled by fire and scarred by* frost and siege. Men must have been afraid of their friends rising up before the due time that they weighted them down with such cruel mounds of masonry.'

Lucia Palk, heroine of the final chapter of this work ('Concerning Lucia'), is buried here. The inscription on her tomb reads, 'Lucia, wife of Robert Palk, daughter of Rev. Dr. Stonehouse. Born Northampton 26th November 1747, Deceased 22nd June 1772. This is followed by twenty lines of verse, ending with:
'The grief will weep and friendship heave a sigh;
Tho wounded memory, the fond tear shall shed;
Yet no fruitless sorrow dim the eye;
To teach the living, lie the sacred dead'

The mortality rate amongst those early inhabitants of Calcutta was dreadful; two monsoons being the popularly estimated average lifespan of new arrivals from the west. The inhospitable climate, malaria and other tropical and little understood diseases, took a fearful toll as did childbirth, poor sanitation and the primitive and uninformed medical care available.

One resident of the early years, Sophia Golborne, recorded in 1785 how the European residents of Calcutta would gather together once the danger period following the monsoon had passed, simply to congratulate each other on having survived. The rapid collapse from life into death is also touched upon by Ms Golborne who spoke of 'a friend is dined with one day and the next is in eternity'.

Children and infants were particularly vulnerable as many of the memorial inscriptions testify: 'Susannah Hunter deceased 7th October 1792 aged 29 years and three of her children who all died in infancy', is typical. Similarly, 'Catherine Sykes deceased 28th December 1786 aged 26 and her stillborn child' or 'Ann Hayes deceased 29th December 1802 aged 24 and two of her infant children' are all too sadly of a pattern.

Conversely, there are some surprising examples of longevity against all the odds: 'Dr Roland Jackson resident here for 32 years died 29th March 1784 having attained 63 years'. No great age by today's standards you may think but to have survived for so long in such an unhealthy climate was then, remarkable.

Others were not so lucky: 'Augustus Cleveland late Collector of Revenues, died 12th January 1784 aged 29, whilst at sea on route for the Cape for recovery of his health'. He is amongst the many recorded as having survived the rigours of Calcutta, being cruelly snatched away whilst travelling home or to a place of convalescence. Others never even reached Calcutta alive: 'Mrs Ann Hayes (clearly another Ann Hayes to that referred to above), died 29th December 1804 aboard the Sir Stephen Lushingston, Indiaman, on route to Calcutta', is typical.

Many of the inscriptions extol at considerable length the many virtues of the deceased, some exhaustively so. Others are brutally graphic: 'Mrs Ann Riley died 1810 after a lingering and painful illness of nine months which she bore with exemplary patience'. Similarly, 'John Lavalin Savage died 30th August 1808, cut off from this world by a malignant disorder'.

There is much 'casting off of mortal coils', 'departing this life', 'called to the maker', esteemed by his fellow officers and men' and so on in this vein. My Bengali friend Udita who accompanied me on what was my latest and her first, visit, was intrigued by this language of a bygone age and use of the long 's' in inscriptions which many mistake for 'f'.

Some inscriptions are cruelly brief on detail: 'Thomas Boileau – born 14th December 1754 died 11th June 1806'. A few more are even bereft of dates, notably, 'Mrs Hersilrige' whose tombstone is set in the wall of the entrance portico.

Other inscriptions seem remarkably indiscrete: 'Robert Cantopher died 18th August 1835, of the Secret and Political Service' or 'James Taylor died 1st October 1839 Assistant of the Secret and Political Department'.

Perhaps the tallest monument in the Cemetery is the dazzlingly whitewashed pyramid tomb of Sir William Jones, polymath and founder of the 'Royal Asiatic Society of Bengal'. This learned Society, now minus the Royal prefix, survives to this day, housed at the other end of Park Street near the Chowringhee crossing. He came to Calcutta in 1783 as a judge of the Supreme Court. A man of formidable intellect, he was a pioneer of modern Indian studies, making the first translations of numerous important works of Indian literature. He died on 27th April 1794 aged just 47 years. The upkeep of his tomb has been funded ever since by the Society he founded.

A close rival in terms of size, is the tomb (also in the form of a pyramid), of Elizabeth Jane Barwell, 'The Celebrated Miss Sanderson' as the inscription reads. She is known to have arrived in Calcutta in 1775, being quickly acclaimed the society beauty of her day and the undisputed belle of Calcutta's grand balls. She had numerous suitors seeking her hand and eventually married Richard Barwell, Calcutta born and bred and a member of the Presidency Council under Warren Hastings. He was also rumoured to be a notorious rake and gambler. Within two years of her marriage and weakened by childbirth and fever, she died on 9th November 1778, 'aged about 23'.

Nearby is the tomb of General Clavering, another member of the Presidency Council under Warren Hastings and his implacable enemy.

Here too rest the mortal remains of Lady Anne Monson, wife of The Hon. Colonel Monson (yet another member of Hasting's Presidency Council). Lady Monson was a great granddaughter of King Charles II. She died in 1775 within a few months of her arrival in Calcutta. Warren Hastings was among the pall bearers of her coffin to the Cemetery gates where it was passed to 'six ladies of noble birth' who bore the coffin the rest of the way to the grave.

Possibly the most unique tomb, taking the form of a Hindu Temple but with a small Islamic dome and replete with carvings of Hindu deities is that of the madly but wonderfully eccentric, Major General Charles Stuart. 'Hindoo Stuart', as he became most widely known, born in 1758, came to India in his teens as an army cadet, rising through the ranks to Major General, commanding his own regiment.

Stuart was one of the very few British to wholeheartedly embrace the Hindu religion and Indian culture. In the words of one contemporary commentator he had 'enthusiastically studied the language, manners and customs of the natives of the country'. He adopted many Indian customs, including daily bathing in the River Hooghly, taking Paan and wearing Indian clothing when off duty.

Stuart's serious convictions as to Hinduism are beyond doubt as are his eccentricities although I cannot entirely shake off the feeling that many of his very public pronouncements were made in frivolity to challenge the conventions of the day; a reaction perhaps to what he may have perceived as the increasing racial arrogance of the more recent European arrivals.

Stuart was a frequent and robust writer of letters to the Calcutta Telegraph newspaper; of the 'outraged of Calcutta' type. He wrote encouraging European ladies to adopt the sari; a suggestion which in the opening years of the nineteenth century, must have been considered outrageous to those at which this unasked for advice was directed. He subsequently published his letters and some of the responses from the less appreciative readers, in a superb volume, exhaustively entitled 'The Ladies' Monitor, Being a Series of Letters First Published in Bengal On the Subject of Female Apparel Tending to Favour a regulated adoption of Indian Costume and Rejection of Superfluous Vesture by the Ladies of the Country With Incidental Remarks on Hindoo Beauty, Whale Bone Stays, Iron Busks, Indian Corsets, Man Milliners, Idle Bachelors, Hair Powder. Waiting Maids and Footmen'; an eclectic mix indeed!

Amongst the reasons he put forward for European ladies to abandon their iron busks was that it made the wearer more susceptible to lightning strike. Perhaps he had a valid point since a small but nevertheless surprising number of those buried in this Cemetery are recorded as having been struck down during electrical storms.

Stuart amassed a considerable collection of sculptures and other idols of Hindu deities which he had shipped to England to form the basis of the British Museum's oriental collection.

Perhaps the most amazing thing Is that Stuart's undoubted eccentricity and outspokenness, given the norms of his day, does not appear to have had any adverse effect upon his career. Today it is difficult to imagine his dissent from the dictated line being tolerated, particularly by the growing numbers ever ready to be offended on behalf of others. Ironically though, much of what Stuart believed and forcefully propounded would now be considered as evidence of an enlightened outlook. What the stiffer elements of his own time made of him though, can only be imagined. I for one would have been delighted to have met him.

Sons of Charles Dickens and Captain Cook are interred here; so too is William Thackeray's father, Richmond. Others include, Henry Chasteney, one time private secretary to Warren Hastings and Lt. Col. Robert Kyd, the distinguished botanist who founded Calcutta's Botanical Gardens, located at Shibpur, a few kilometres downriver from the Howrah Bridge.

The observant will have noticed 'S.O. fecit' discretely inscribed on many of the tombs. This is the mark of Samuel Oldham, the first undertaker in Bengal. He is buried here but his grave along with others was levelled in the nineteenth century. His memorial stone however, was preserved and, along with others, is set in the walls of the entrance portico.

One of the best known and most frequently visited tombs is that of Rose Aylmer; marked by a graceful spiral fluted column, broken off to symbolise a sudden and untimely death.

Rose Aylmer was, fleetingly, the teenaged inamorata of the poet, William Savage Landor. Within a year of her arrival in Calcutta, she succumbed to cholera in the outbreak of 1800, aged just twenty years. Landor was reportedly devastated by her death, composing a poem in her memory, the following part of which was later inscribed on the base of her tomb:
'Ah, what awaits the sceptred race!
Ah, what the form divine!
What every virtue, every grace
Rose Aylmer, all were thine…'

It is rarely that I will spend less than two hours on my visits to the Cemetery, sometimes considerably longer. It is very easy to become completely immersed in all that is around you and no matter how many previous visits, you always seem to discover something not previously seen.

First time visitors often remark on the level of decay affecting many of the monuments. Two and a half centuries of Calcutta's unforgiving climate having obliterated many inscriptions and given a moth eaten appearance to many of the monuments by exposing parts of their underlying brick structure. Up until a few decades ago, it was all very much worse. By the 1970's the Cemetery had sunk to a deplorable condition, with squatters occupying any vacant space and indeed even some of the open fronted memorials. Rubbish was everywhere with stray dogs and even a few cows, nosing about between the graves.

The Christian Burial Board has brought about huge improvements to the Cemetery which is now unrecognisable to that I first visited all those years ago. A great deal of sympathetic restoration to the monuments has been undertaken and a great deal more is in progress. Most of the collapsed headstones and memorial plaques have been reset, either vertically in the eastern boundary wall or horizontally adjacent to some of the pathways. Given the limited financial and manpower resources available to the Board, its achievements have been quite remarkable.

Quite nearby the South Park Street Cemetery are two others used over the centuries for Christian burials but although neither of these are anywhere near the same stamp they are certainly worth a mention.

The first of these cemeteries is the General Episcopal Cemetery but which is more widely known as the Lower Circular Road (now AJC Bose) Road cemetery. This can be found north of the South Park Street Cemetery along the eastern side of AJC Bose Road, just before the sprawling Beniapuker Tram Depot.

This cemetery was founded in 1797 by Edward Tiretta (who also gave his name to Tiretta Bazar, just off Rabindra Sarani adjacent to the New CIT Road junction). He was a political refugee from Italy and after settling in Calcutta, held the post of Superintendent of Streets and Buildings for many years. Originally, Tiretta's new cemetery was to be for Catholics only; it was only later that the burial of non-Catholics was permitted. Tiretta's wife, Angelica, was amongst the first to occupy the cemetery having been reinterred here in 1797, a year after her death.

Unlike South Park Street Cemetery, this burial ground is still in use and the front section, nearest AJC Bose Road, is relatively clear and reasonably well kept. The older graves are to be found further east and around the perimeter of the extensive grounds. These areas are in a deplorable condition; so badly overgrown that graves without vertical memorials are no longer visible. The cemetery staff are helpful chaps and if asked (and for a modest consideration), will use their crowbars to prise back the creepers and other vegetation to allow an inspection of the many graves hidden in the undergrowth.

The second of these cemeteries is the Scottish Cemetery, still proudly announced in the arched ironwork nameplate surmounting the main entrance.

This cemetery can be found east of the South Park Street Cemetery, sandwiched between Park Street and Shakespeare Sarani and occupying an area of land between Karaya Row and Mrgendra Lal Mitra Road. The main entrance is accessed from Gorosthan Lane.

The Scottish Cemetery was established in 1820, extended in 1858 and from then until the 1940's was the principal burial ground for generations of Calcutta based Scots and other members of the congregation of St Andrew's Church. The iron entrance gates are usually padlocked, visitors being rare. Just give the gates a good rattle to alert the resident caretaker and he will let you in.

As you enter the Cemetery through an attractive, ochre washed gatehouse, you are met immediately with a scene of desolation. Amongst the undergrowth are hundreds of monuments in every stage of decay and collapse; toppled or leaning drunkenly, split apart or strangled by creepers. Some are so overgrown that they cannot be detected until you are literally standing on top of them.

Amidst all this apparent neglect, there is clear evidence that some attempt is made on a regular basis to prevent the Cemetery grounds from reverting entirely to jungle. In 2008, a major clearance of the Cemetery was undertaken under the auspices of the Calcutta Scottish Heritage Trust, in order to conduct a site investigation. The objective was to assess the extent, condition and history of the site and its monuments. Since then little further significant action seems to have been taken. So far as I can ascertain there is only the resident caretaker and one old gardener to keep the encroaching vegetation at bay. Although they strive to do the best they can, the task is quite beyond such slim resources.

The Caretaker keeps some records which can be examined upon request. There is the inevitable visitors' book to sign and in which you can include your comments. One small word of warning. There are a couple of local drunks who have hit upon the idea of 'guiding' western visitors around the Cemetery for a fee, naturally. They will suddenly present themselves whenever they see a visitor approaching. Of course they know absolutely nothing about the Cemetery but do understand when told to get lost.

Chapter 28

CALCUTTA IN A DAY

'What can I see of Calcutta in a day?' It is a question I have so often been asked. 'Well very little really' had tended to be my stock response. This admittedly negative reaction had become almost automatic but the repeated question did set me thinking about a more constructive answer to the traveller with serious time constraints.

So many travellers come to Calcutta in transit to somewhere else; few will choose the City as their final destination or will stay longer than a few days. The main disadvantage for the short stay traveller is that they have little opportunity of coming to terms with the City; of acclimatising to the hectic, pullulating, cacophonous battle of life that is Calcutta in full swing. I have always taken the view that if the traveller has the opportunity to gain some first-hand understanding of how the City works, they will leave with a more positive impression and perhaps be encouraged to return for a longer stay.

Having given the matter some thought, I make the following suggestions which I hope can provide the time limited traveller with a snapshot of Calcutta in all its many and various aspects. All involve the use of public transport, details of which are given. Whilst correct at the time of writing, transport routes can change. Accordingly, I have included telephone numbers and email addresses so that the reader may check at the time of travel.

For trams, general enquiries can be made by telephone (033) 8697733391/2 or go to www.calcuttatramways.com.

By Tram, River Ferry and on foot:

This suggestion follows a route from central to north Calcutta by tram; from there to Howrah by river ferry then on foot across the Howrah Bridge and along MG Road to the CR Avenue crossing.

Start from the Tram Depot at Esplanade at the northern end of Chowringhee. Here you pick up tram, route number 12/7 bound for Galiff Street in north Calcutta. This tram route may sometimes be signed Baghbazar rather than Galiff Street; no matter the destination is the same.

Your destination is the Baghbazar ferry ghat, (located a few minutes before the tram terminates at Galiff Street) where you will take the River ferry to Howrah.

The 12/7 tram operates between 5.50 am and 9.00 pm with an average frequency of about twenty minutes. The fare is five rupees per head. The route is approximately seven kilometres and runs via Dalhousie Square, Bentinck Street and the entire length of Rabindra Sarani (erstwhile Chitpore Road, which I will allow myself the liberty of using here). The Chitpore Road once had either an Upper (north) or Lower (south) prefix and you will still see this on the nameplates of some commercial premises along the thoroughfare.

The Chitpore Road is arguably the best thoroughfare in which to observe the frenetic and relentless dynamism of Calcutta at its most atmospheric. Here you will find wholesalers and retailers of shoes and chappals, of clothing of every description, wig makers, perfumers, idol carvers in stone and wood, tinsmiths, ironmongers, traders in brightly coloured plastic buckets and brooms, printers of posters and calendars and a multitude of pavement hawkers in fruit, vegetables, razor blades, padlocks, combs and brushes, earbuds and other personal requisites. The narrow footpaths and roadway will be filled beyond capacity with pedestrians, with or without impossible loads, rickshaw and cart pullers, smoking and battered buses, trucks and every other form of motorised traffic and clanking trams; all jostling for a way forward.

Ask the tram conductor to alert you when the tram reaches the stop for Baghbazar. For the ferry ghat, cross the tracks of the Circular Railway to your left and walk straight on until you hit the River. The ticket office is located just to the left of the ramp which leads down to the ferry landing stage. The fare to Howrah will be six rupees and fifty paise. Retain your ticket which you will need to hand in when you disembark at Howrah. The ramshackle ferries run at approximate twenty to twenty five minute intervals and are an essential experience for all travellers to Calcutta.

The ferry to Howrah takes about twenty minutes or so including the two stops en route, first at Sovabazar Ghat then at Ahriatola Ghat, within sight of the great iron Howrah Bridge. This gives you plenty of time to take in all that is going on around you. As the passengers pile aboard, so will a coterie of itinerant small traders and service providers. There will be the seller of nuts and other small snacks; the shoe clean man with his wooden box, brushes and polish and sometimes, an ear cleaning practitioner with his wallet of gruesome looking instruments with which he will remove wax from the ears of his clients. If you are really lucky there will be entertainment laid on by as migrant lady with a squeezebox type instrument and a small child doing an accompanying dance routine passing themselves through a small iron hoop.

Heading downriver towards the Bridge, most of the activity will be taking place to your left on the eastern bank. You will pass a number of bathing ghats and both the Kashi Mitra and Nimtola burning ghats. Don't forget that the view of the Howrah Bridge from midstream on the ferry is just about as good as it gets.

When the ferry docks at Howrah Ghat, the ferry ramp leads up to the ticket hall. Outside, turn right and head up the slight incline in the direction of the Howrah Bridge. Details of the Bridge and what you can expect to see there are given at chapter 26.

On reaching the eastern (Calcutta) end of the Bridge, go to the right until you see a pedestrian crossing manned by a white uniformed traffic policeman. This takes you across Strand Road, under the Brabourne Road Flyover, into the western end of MG Road.

Walk east along MG Road, using either pavement; both being equally teeming and 'scenic'. So congested and obstructed are the pavements of this madly busy thoroughfare that many stretches can only be successfully negotiated by taking to the roadway.

By the time you reach the major junction with CR Avenue you will have compressed into the few hours it has taken you since setting out, more of the Calcutta experience than many travellers will ever gain. From the busy CR Avenue junction, MG Road Metro station is about a ten minute walk to your left whilst Central Metro station is an approximate fifteen minute walk to the right.

Calcutta by Tram:

Trams are an integral part of Calcutta's heritage. Tram transport in the City began way back in the last quarter of the nineteenth century with a horse drawn affair running from Sealdah, along BB Ganguly Street to the Armenian Ghat. This was later updated with a steam locomotive being employed to haul the tramcars. In 1900, the system was electrified.

Described as a lifeline of the City, Calcutta's present tram network employs an average of 170 trams running at any one time, over approximately 70 kilometres of double track, beginning at 4.15 am and shutting down at 11.40 pm. To me, for getting across the City there is no better option than the tram.

The excellent Calcutta Tramways Company now run City Joy Rides in a modern air conditioned tram covering the following three routes:

Esplanade to Khidepur return, via Maiden and Garden Reach Road;

Esplanade to Shyambazar return, via Lenin Sarani, Nirmal Chandra Street, College Street and Bidhan Sarani;

Esplanade to Kalighat return, via Maidan, Alipore Road, Hazra Road and SP Mukherjee Road.

Pre booking starts from six days prior to the date of the intended journey. This can be done either in person at Esplanade Tram Depot ticket counter (10.30 am to 5.00 pm weekdays and 7.00 am and 5.00 pm on weekends and holidays), or by telephoning the booking counter on (033) 8697733475.

Precise details of days timings and fares as follows:

Days on which all three routes operate are Wednesdays, Saturdays and Sundays plus all public holidays;

Timings and fares are:

Esplanade to Khidepur return – Departs Esplanade 5.00 pm. Fare is 100 Rupees.

Esplanade to Shyambazar return – Departs Esplanade at 9.00 am. Fare is 150 Rupees.

Esplanade to Kalighat return – Departs Esplanade 3.00 pm. Fare is 150 Rupees.

Chapter 29

CALCUTTA'S MARKETS

Markets the world over provide one of the best insights into the way life is lived locally. Nowhere is this truer than in teeming Calcutta.

A number of Calcutta's markets have been covered in preceding chapters. Those which have not, are listed below together with details of their locations.

Hogg (New) Market:

Lindsey Street, between Fenwick Bazar Street and Bertram Street. Nearest Metro station is Esplanade, then a five minute walk south along Chowringhee, turning eastward along Lindsey Street.

Chandni Chawk Market:

Chandni Chawk Street at the junction with Lenin Sarani. The nearest Metro station is Chandni Chawk then a five minute walk eastwards along Ganesh Chandra Avenue, turning southwards into Chadni Chawk Street.

Nandaram Market:

Brabourne Road at junction with Basanta Lal Murarka Street. The nearest Metro stations, MG Road/Central are more than twenty minutes' walk distant. A taxi is recommended.

Bagri Market:

Canning Street at the junction with Amratola Street. The transport options are as for Nandaram Market above.

Yhudi Market:

Bidhan Sarani between Keshab Sen Street and Bechu Chatterjee Street. The nearest Metro station is MG Road, then a five minute walk eastwards along Madan Mohan Burman Street, turning north into Bidhan Sarani.

Srimani Market:

Bidhan Sarani at the junction with Sarkar Lane. The nearest Metro station is Girish Park then a ten minute walk eastwards along Vivekananda Road, turning south into Bidhan Sarani.

Shyambazar Market:

Bidhan Sarani at the junction with Bhupen Bose Avenue, just east of the five point crossing. The nearest Metro station is Shyambazar, almost adjacent.

Posta Market:

Kali Krishna Tagore Street at the junction with Strand Road. The Market sprawls both north and south of this location. The nearest Metro station is Girish Park, then a fifteen minute walk westwards along Vivekananda Road and Kali Krishna Tagore Street.

Hatibagan Market:

Hatibagan Crossing. Bidhan Sarani at the junction with Sri Arabinda Sarani. The nearest Metro station is Sovabazar, then a ten minute walk eastwards along Sri Arabinda Sarani.

Maniktala Market:

APC (Circular) Road at the junction with Vivekananda Road. The nearest Metro station is Girish Park, then a fifteen minute walk eastwards along Vivekananda Road.

Muchibazar Market:

Ultadanga Main Road at the junction with Ariff Road. Travel there by taxi is recommended.

Ultadanga Municipal Market:

Ultadanga Main Road, just west of the junction with Gurudas Dutta Gardens. Travel there by taxi is recommended.

Bagmari Market:

Maniktala Main Road, just east of the Vivekananda Bridge over the Circular Canal. Travel there by taxi is recommended.

Entally Market:

Eastern side of APC (Circular) Road between Girish Chandra Bose Road and Dr L Mohan Bhattacharji Road. Travel there by taxi is recommended.

Kalighat Market:

Western side of Kalighat Road, approximately two hundred metres north of Kali Temple Road. The Kalighat Metro station serving the area is a good fifteen minute walk distant. From the station, walk westwards along Chetla Central Road, turning north into Kalighat Road; the Market being five hundred metres on, to the left.

Chapter 30

OTHER PLACES OF INTEREST

The Victoria Memorial:
Walking southward across the Maidan after daybreak on a Calcutta 'winter' day you will see in the distance and nearly enveloped in early morning mist, a huge white domed building seeming to float above the distant treeline. Unfortunately, you can get this similar magical effect most summer afternoons but then this will be due to pollution not mist. This is the Victoria Memorial or Victoria Memorial Hall to give it its correct name.

Located at the southern end of the Maidan, off Chowringhee (or Jaharlalal Nehru Road as that section has been renamed), the Memorial is the grandest edifice in Calcutta by far: it was meant to be, that was the intention of its creator, Lord Curzon, when Viceroy of India.

Lord Curzon first proposed building a grand memorial in 1901 following the death of the Queen Empress although the foundation stone was not laid until 1906, the year after Curzon left India. The Memorial was not finally completed until 1921, some nine years since Calcutta had ceased to be the capital of India; this honour having been transferred to Delhi in 1912.

The Memorial's architect was William Emerson and it was constructed by Messrs. Martin and Co. of Calcutta. Built in white Makrana marble with a huge central dome and four subsidiary domes, it represents an eclectic mix of architectural styles perhaps best described as Indo Saracenic revivalist with Venetian, Egyptian and Islamic stylistic influences.

Mounted atop the Memorial's central dome is the 4.9 metre figure of the Angel of Victory. Set around this dome are allegorical sculptures depicting art, architecture, Justice and charity. Above the north porch are motherhood, prudence and learning.

Within the Memorial Hall there are a number of galleries showing a collection of royal portraits and visual displays, charting the history of the development of Calcutta. At one time these displays were rather haphazard but have been improved considerably in recent years.

Set in beautiful and well maintained gardens with pleasing water features, the Memorial is very well visited not only by western travellers but by many visitors to Calcutta from all over the sub-continent, many of whom will often ask you to pose with them for photographs.

The Memorial Hall is open Tuesdays to Sundays inclusive, from 10.00 am until 7.00 pm

The nearest Metro station is Maidan, just a short stroll away.

St. Paul's Cathedral:

Quite close to the Victoria Memorial, at the southernmost extremity of the Maidan, is the grandest of all Calcutta's churches, St. Paul's Cathedral.

The original Cathedral was built between 1839 and 1847, to a design by the military engineer, Major William Nairns Forbes.

The original tower and spire is said to have been based on that of Norwich Cathedral. Alterations were made to the Cathedral following the great cyclone of 1864 and again following earthquake damage in 1897. A further earthquake caused the collapse of the tower. This was rebuilt but along the lines of the Bell Harry Tower at Canterbury Cathedral.

Within the Cathedral there are some particularly finely carved pews and an alter screen. There is also some notable stained glass; that in the west window, in memory to Lord Mayo, being to a design by Sir Edward Burne Jones. It is also within the Cathedral where most of the memorials are to be found.

The Cathedral is open every day between 10.00 am and 7.00 pm but annoyingly, is shut to visitors daily between 12 noon and 3.00 pm.

The nearest Metro station is Maidan, which is close by and in sight of the Cathedral.

The Indian Museum:
The Indian Museum, almost certainly the oldest in the sub-continent, had its origins in the collections of the (then Royal) Asiatic Society of Bengal founded by Sir William Jones in 1784.

The Museum was created in the early years of the nineteenth century as a place 'where manmade and natural objects could be collected, cared for and displayed'.

The magnificent building in which the Museum is now housed, dates from 1875 and is to a design by Walter R Granville. In recent years the building has undergone considerable renovation.

The Museum houses an eclectic mix covering art, archaeology, geology, botany, zoology and anthropology. There is a four thousand year old Egyptian mummy, skeletons of prehistoric animals and other fossils, meteorites and, it is claimed the Buddha's ashes.

The Museum is located in Chowringhee, just south of the junction with Park Street; the Metro station of that name being close by.

The Museum is open Tuesdays to Sundays inclusive from 10.00 am until 5.00 pm.

The Ochterlony Monument:
This slender, graceful Ochterlony Monument is sited at the north eastern corner of the Maidan, just behind Esplanade (which is the nearest Metro station) and adjacent to the City's long distance bus terminus.

Erected from public funds in 1829, the Monument is to the memory of the flamboyant Major General Sir David Ochterlony, to celebrate the successful defence of Delhi against the Marathas in 1804 and the victory of the East India Company's armed forces in the Anglo Nepalese War.

In that special Indian way of obliterating historical connection by changing a name, in 1969 it was decided that the Monument be renamed Shaheed Minar (Martyrs Monument) in memory of the martyrs of the independence struggle.

The Monument is forty eight metres high, with two viewing balconies. In 1991, a foreign tourist fell, or flung themselves from the first of these two balconies. As a consequence, admission has been severely restricted ever since.

The architectural style of the Monument in Islamic with a mix of Egyptian, Syrian and Turkish influences; the overall result is delightful. In recent years a great deal of restoration work has been undertaken, including floodlighting, to excellent effect.

The Monument has always been a rallying point for political protest with often huge crowds gathered in the surrounding open space. In the bad old days of the 1970's such protest often spiralled into howling riot, leaving the area wreathed in the mist of tear gas.

The Marble Palace:
Wandering the pullulating lanes and gullees of Chor Bagan (literally 'Thieves Garden'), the area between Beadon Street and Rabindra Sarani, just north of Mechua Bazar, you will come across just about the most unlikely building you would expect to find.

Here at number 46 Muktarum Babu Street is the Marble Palace. Set well back from the Street amidst beautiful gardens and behind classical high iron railings and gates, this magnificently eccentric building, simply stops you in your tracks. Given the uniqueness and sheer scale of the Palace, it has always struck me as just so Indian that those who decide such matters, perceived the need to identify the place by allocating to it a street number. I am rather glad they did.

Built in the neoclassical style by Raja Rajendra Mullick, between 1835 and 1840, this graceful mansion takes its name from the ninety (it is said) varieties of marble which adorn its floors, panelled walls and staircases. Looking from the gateway across the gardens, complete with statuary and Italianate fountain, to the Palaces pale grey Palladian frontage, it is difficult to believe you are still in Calcutta and have not somehow been magically transported to some quiet corner of Rome or Florence.

Within, the Palace is even more surprising. Giving every appearance of a madly overstocked museum, it was until quite

OTHER PLACES OF INTEREST

recently, the family home of the Mullicks. The enormous collections of sculpture, furniture, clocks, mirrors, chandeliers, porcelain, pottery and glassware, are all objects collected over the years by generations of the family in its frequent travels around the globe. Amongst the collection of paintings, there are significant works by Reubens and Sir Joshua Reynolds.

The Palace is open to visitors every day except Tuesdays and Thursdays, between 10.00 am and 4.00 pm. Perversely, it is necessary first to obtain a ticket of entry at least one day in advance of your proposed visit. You obtain this from the Government of India Tourist Office, located at 4 Shakespeare Sarani, just off the southern end of Chowringheee; Maidan being the nearest Metro station.

The nearest Metro station to the Marble Palace is MG Road. From there a few minutes' walk northwards and Muktarum Babu Street is to the left.

The Tagore Museum:
Popularly known as the Jorasanko Thakur Bari (the house of the Thakurs, anglicized to Tagore, in the Jorasanko area of north Calcutta). This is the ancestral home of the distinguished and multi-talented Tagore family. It is where India's first Nobel Laureate, Rabindranath Tagore, was born in 1861 and where he died eighty years later.

The house, which is now within and forms part of, the Rabindra Bharati University, was built by Dwarkinath Tagore (Rabindra's grandfather), in 1785. It was subsequently altered substantially; parts even being demolished. Now restored to reflect how it would have been when inhabited by the family, it now serves as the Tagore Museum.

The Museum is a major repository of the works of the Tagores in the form of manuscripts, paintings, books and photographs depicting the history of the family and its involvement in the Bengali religious and cultural renaissance.

The Museum is open between 10.00 am and 5.00 pm on weekdays and to 1.30 pm on Saturdays. There is also an excellent forty minute light and sound show, staged in English on weekdays, commencing 7.00 pm (November to January) and 8.00 pm (February to June). Well worth attending.

The Museum is located at 6 Dwarkinath Tagore Lane (off Madan Mohan Chatterjee Lane) The Museum may also be accessed through the grand arched gateway, direct from Rabindra Sarani.

The nearest Metro stations are MG Road and Girish Park, each approximately equidistant from the Museum. From MG Road station walk northwards up CR Avenue, taking the second main turning on your left into Madan Chatterjee Lane. From Girish Park station, walk southwards down CR Avenue and Madan Chatterjee Lane is the second turning on the right once past the busy Vivekananda Road junction.

The Calcutta Police Museum:
The Calcutta Police Museum is administered by the Calcutta Police and is a woefully unpublicised gem.

This marvellous Museum can be found on the western side of APC (Upper Circular) Road at number 113. This is also the office of Calcutta's Deputy Commissioner of Police; the Museum being housed in one of the several handsome buildings making up this gated complex. It is a must for any traveller interested in Calcutta's history.

The grandeur of the buildings forming this complex is explained by the fact that from 1814 until 1830, they formed the principal residence of Raja Ram Mohan Roy; denoted on a plaque set in the front boundary wall.

OTHER PLACES OF INTEREST

On arrival, you will need to report to the guard house located just inside the compound gateway. Once cleared, walk straight ahead to the building housing the Museum; this being set a little further back in the well kept grounds. The Museum is open every day except Mondays, between 11.00 am and 5.00 pm. No advance booking is required.

Housed on two floors, the well planned and presented displays, trace the organisation and development of the Calcutta Police from the earliest days of the eighteenth century to the present day. The displays include notes on celebrated cases together with related exhibits from the Police investigations. Many of the most famous cases relate to the freedom struggle against British rule and have considerable historical significance. To those travellers who have journeyed as far as Port Blair in India's far flung Andaman Islands and visited the Cellular Jail there, some of the names recorded in the Police Museum exhibits, will strike a familiar chord. Port Blair's Cellular Jail is where many of those convicted freedom fighters served out their sentences. Interestingly, well over ninety percent of those recorded as having been incarcerated in that island jail for offences related to the freedom struggle, were Bengalis.

Amongst the displays are included copies of numerous directives issued by long dead Commissioners of Police. Many give a sideways glance at the development of the social norms of Calcutta down the centuries. My favourites include those urging police officers to take tougher action against such anti-social activities as 'kite flying' and 'furious driving' (of carriages) in the Bow Bazar area.

On the staircase to the upper floor displays, stands the twisted casing of a World War II, Japanese bomb dropped on Hattibagan bazar but which, thankfully, failed to explode.

To get to the Police Museum it is easiest to take a taxi; the Museum being some distance from any convenient Metro station. For those wishing to use the Metro, get out at Girish Park station. Head eastwards along Vivekananda Road, crossing the major junctions with Bidhan Sarani and Amherst Street before reaching APC Road. At this very busy junction, the Maniktala Market is over to your left; its pleasing domed clock tower being something of a landmark. For the Police Museum, turn right into APC Road and it will be found about two hundred metres south, to your right and almost opposite the Calcutta Leprosy Mission Hospital.

The Jain Temple:

The Pareshnath Jain Temple is dedicated to the tenth of the twenty four Jain Tirthunkar Seetalnathji. Built in 1867 by a prominent Mawari Jain jeweller, Rui Bahadur Badridas.

The Temple complex, which actually contains four separate Temples, stands in beautifully kept flower gardens complete with a stream, fountain and well stocked fish pond. The gardens also contain intricate mosaics, worked in tile, glass and stone, many of quite exquisite design.

The Temple structures themselves are highly ornate; richly ornamented with inlaid mirror and other glasswork. There are a number of beautifully crafted windows in stained glass and some magnificent chandeliers. The complex also contains a small museum.

The Temple complex is located in Badridas Temple Street in north Calcutta, east of APC Road and adjacent to the west bank of the Circular Canal.

A taxi is the easiest way to get to the Temple as the nearest Metro stations, Girish Park and Sovabazar are both a good thirty minute walk distant.

Temple timings are 6.00 am to 11.30 am and 3.00 pm to 7.00 pm, daily.

OTHER PLACES OF INTEREST

The Botanical Gardens:

The Botanical Gardens are located on the west bank of the River Hooghly at Shibpur, approximately four kilometres south of the Vidyasagar Setu (Bridge).

Originally called 'The Honourable (East India) Company's Botanic Garden in Calcutta', it was officially renamed in 2009 with the equally exhaustive, 'Acharya Jagadish Chandra Bose Indian Botanical Garden'.

Covering an area approaching 109 hectares, the Gardens began to be laid out by the East India Company in 1787, under the direction of Colonel Robert Kyd, a noted botanist of his day. The Gardens were further developed by William Roxburgh, another noted botanist who became Superintendent of the Gardens from 1793.

The Gardens are an absolute haven of tranquillity after the relentless pandemonium of the City; somewhere to recharge your batteries.

Within the Gardens there are lakes and water lily ponds, boasting giant lilies up to one and a half metres in diameter, thousands of perennial plants and rare tree species, all beautifully maintained.

The star attraction is the famous 250 year old giant Banyan tree, with a circumference of 330 metres and boasting one of the largest canopies in nature.

The Gardens are open to the public on all days throughout the year from 9.30 am to 6.00 pm.

At one time, you could get to the Botanical Garden by River ferry from Chandpal Ghat. Unfortunately this service was discontinued some years back. Now, by far the easiest way to get there is by taxi.

Kalighat:

Kalighat is an area of the City to the south east of the Alipur Central Jail and sandwiched between Tolly's Nullah to the west and the major thoroughfare of Shyam Prasad (SP) Mukherjee Road to the east.

People will come to Kalighat for two reasons, well three actually if you include the thriving but down market red light area there. Firstly, the famous Kali Temple, visited by pilgrims from all over India and beyond. Secondly, Nirmal Hriday (Sacred Heart), the home for the dying, established by Mother Theresa way back in 1952 and located, ironically, right next door to the Temple.

Kalighat is well served by public transport, with a Metro station of that name located at SP Mukherjee Road. The presence of the Temple and the daily throng of pilgrims gives the whole area a kind of perpetual festival air. This is intensified by the congregating hordes of hawkers in anything from Temple offerings of fruit, flowers and what have you, to fridge magnets and posters depicting Hindu deities. You will in all likelihood even see a variety of tee shirts on offer as a souvenir of your visit.

The Temple, as the name suggests, is dedicated to the goddess Kali, whose nightmarish image with frightening eyes, lolling tongue dripping blood, a neck entwined with snakes and garlanded with a string of skulls, is to be seen all over Calcutta, particularly during the major Kali festival held annually in October/November.

The present Temple building dates from 1809 and is said to have replaced a much earlier one. The origins of this as a site of worship are to be found in Hindu mythology which says this is the place where the little toe of the Goddess fell to earth when her body, carried by Shiva, was cut into fifty two pieces by Lord

OTHER PLACES OF INTEREST

Vishnu's chakra (a kind of flying saw). Wherever the fifty two body parts landed became a place of pilgrimage.

The squeamish should avoid the south end of the Temple where goats are offered for sacrifice.

You should note that non Hindus have only very limited access to the Temple confines. Temple timings are from 6.00 am to 2.00 pm and 5.00 pm to 9.00 pm.

Next door to the Temple is Nirmal Hriday, opened in 1952 by Mother Theresa and her original twelve fellow Missionaries of Charity for the care of the destitute dying. Their work went virtually unheralded, certainly in the west, until the late 1960's when a succession of western television journalists travelled to Calcutta to report on the work being undertaken there. Whilst broadcasting footage of the faces of the dying could certainly be considered to be inappropriate and in questionable taste, it did succeed in pricking the collective conscience of the west, setting in train an influx of donations for the work of the Order. Unfortunately, is also did much to create an impression of Calcutta, in the minds of the many who would never travel there, as a place of unspeakable human degradation. Regrettably, this was later reinforced by subsequent commentators and seekers of those 'images of horror' so that the very name Calcutta became a metaphor for all that was terrifyingly awful. Many Bengalis felt justifiably aggrieved that almost no attempt had been made in these portrayals to give fair balance by also reporting on the other and more positive aspects of the City.

Nirmal Hriday was the forerunner in the Order's services to Calcutta's poorest of the poor. This house for the destitute dying was followed by the setting up of several further havens; Shanti Nagar, for lepers and Nirmala Shishu Bhavan, a children's home, to name just two.

The Mother House of the Order, where Mother Theresa was buried, is located on AJC Bose (Lower Circular) Road just by the junction with Abdul Halim Lane.

Since the early days of the 1950's, the Order has grown considerably. On your wanderings around the City, keep a look out for these wonderful ladies, easily identifiable by their blue bordered, simple white saris.

Glossary

Aakh wallah	sugar cane grinder
Agarbatti	incense sticks
Aloo	potato
Anglo-Indian	Indian of mixed blood
Angrezi	English
Ashram	place of religious retreat
Auto-rickshaw	3 wheeled two stroke motorised taxi
Babu	clerk or bureaucrat
Bagh	garden
Baniya	shopkeeper or trader
Baapu	Mahatma Ghandi (lit. father)
Beedie	thin hand rolled poor man's cigarette
Bhaji	fried vegetables
Bhand	small earthenware cup
Bheestie	traditional water carrier
Bisleri	bottled water
Bonti	Static blade used in food preparation
Brahmin	highest caste
Burra	big or senior
Bustee	registered slum
Chabbi wallah	key maker
Chackra	kind of flying saw (archaic)

Chai	tea
Chaikhana	tea stall
Chapatti	thin Indian flatbread
Chappals	sandals
Charpoy	rope sprung bed
Charpresi	messenger
Chawl	tenement slum (more west India)
Chowk (Chawk)	market
Chowkidar	watchman or gatekeeper
Chota	small or junior
Countrymade	Illegally made (e.g. liquor, firearm etc)
Chula	cooking stove, wood or dung fuelled
Dada	gang leader, hoodlum.
Dal	dish of lentils or other pulses
Dalits	lowest castes (lit. the oppressed)
Darwan	gatekeeper
Devi	goddess
Dhobi	laundry
Dhoti	traditional Hindu men's loincloth
Doms	members of the caste who handle dead bodies
Dosa	plain or spicy rice flower pancake
Dupatta	scarf worn with salwar kameez
Durga	Hindu deity representing benevolent side of power
Eve	woman or women
Eve teasing	sexual harassment of females
Firang	foreign
Firinghee	foreigner
Ful jharu	long feather duster cleaning stick

GLOSSARY

Ghat	steps to bathing or landing place on river
Ghee	clarified butter widely used in cooking
Godown	warehouse
Goonda	thug, criminal lout
Gunny	sack
Gupshup	to gossip
Harijan	untouchable castes (lit. children of God)
Havaldar	police rank between constable/inspector
Hijra	member of a group of eunuchs
Holi	Hindu spring festival of colours
Idly (Idli)	rice flower dumpling, breakfast dish usually served with sambhar
Jaggery	unrefined coarse sugar
Jawan	soldier
Ji	respectful suffix to name, e.g. Gandhiji
Kali	Hindu deity representing the darker side of power
Karma	fate or destiny
Katra	sub division of a market
Khadi	hand woven cloth
Kothi	same as Katra above
Kshatriya	warrior caste
Kumar	potter caste
Kurta	man's long loose shirt
Kutcha	rough, crude, unsophisticated
Lathi	Bamboo stave tipped with iron used By police and chowkidars

Mahajan	money lender
Maidan	parkland or grassed open space
Masala	mixture of spices used to flavour food
Masala dosa	folded pancake with spiced veg. filling
Masjid	Mosque
Naan	Indian flatbread cooked in tandoor oven
Namaskar	Hindu word of greeting
Nimbu	lemon or lime
Nirvana	spiritual enlightenment
Paan	folded leaf with spiced Araca nut or other fillings, including tobacco, a stimulant
Pandit (Pundit)	Hindu scholar
Pani	water
Paratha	Indian flatbread fried in ghee
Patti	sub division of a market
Puja	religious devotions
Pukka	good, sound, correct
Puri	small puffed breads fried in ghee
Rickshaw	hand pulled, wheeled small carriage
Roti	Indian bread
Sabzi	vegetable
Sadhu	Hindu holy man
Sag	spinach
Sambhar	masala lentil sauce
Sardar	chief, boss, leader
Salwar kameez	women's costume of long blouse and loose trousers

GLOSSARY

Sati	now outlawed tradition of widow burning
Sepoy	Indian foot soldier
Shaan wallah	knife grinder
Shishi bottle wallah	scavenger of plastic bottles
Shri	respectful prefix to name
Tank	artificial water reservoir
Tempo	large 3 wheeled motorised vehicle
Thali	veg. or non veg. set lunch meal
Tiffin	light snack or luncheon
Tilak	Hindu sacred forehead mark
Untouchables	the 'scheduled' or lowest castes
Upanishads	Hindu scriptures
Vaishya	traditional trading caste
Wallah	man e.g. dhobi wallah = laundry man
Wojon wallah	man in the street with bathroom scales on which you can weigh yourself for a fee.
Yogi	Hindu ascetic
Zamindar	major landlord
Zarda	a form of cut tobacco often mixed in paan
Zindabad	lit. 'long live' much used at political rallies

Old and New Street Names

Old Name	New Name
Amherst Street	Raja Rammohan Sarani
Arpuli Lane	Surendralal Pyne Lane
Auckland Road	Sahid Khudiram Bose Road
Auckland Square	Benjamin Moloire Square
Baitakkhanna 1st Lane	Debendra Nath Roy Lane
Banamali Sarkar Street	Gopeswar Pal Street
Bancharam Arkur Lane	Dhiren Dhar Sarani
Banerjee Bagan Lane	Banerjee Bagan Road
Banstala Street	Sir Hariram Goenka Street
Basak Dighi Lane	Kedar Banerjee Lane
Basak Lane	Gurudas Basak Lane
Beadon Street (part)	Ahbedandra Road
Beadon Street (part)	Dani Ghosh Sarani
Beadon Square	Rabindra Kanan
Belgachia Road	Khudiram Bose Sarani
Beliaghata Main Road	Dr Suresh Ch. Benerji Road
Beniapukur Road	Hare Krishna Konar Road
Biren Roy Road	Raja Rammohan Road
Blacquire Square	Sadhak Ramprasad Udyan
Bosepara Lane (part)	Ma Saradamoni Lane
Bowbazar Street	B.B. Ganguly Street
Bowpara Lane	Gopi Sen Lane

OLD AND NEW STREET NAMES

Old Name	New Name
Brabourne Road	Biplabi Trailokya Maharaj Road
British Indian Street	Abdul Hamil Street
Calvert Road	Nafar Koley Road
Canning Street	Biplabi Rash Behari Bose Road
Carmac Street	Abanindra Nath Thakur Sarani
Cathedral Road	Herasim Labedeff Sarani
Charnock Place	Netaji Subhas Road
Charakdanga Road	Kabi Sukanta Sarani
Chitpur Road (Upper & Lower)	Rabindra Sarani
Chitpur Bridge Approach	Mohit Moitra Sarani
Chor Bagan Lane	Amar Bose Sarani
Chowringhee (part)	Jawaharlal Nehru Road
Chutapara Lane	Harish Sikdar Path
Clive Ghat Street	Narendra Ch. Dutta Sarani
Clive Row	Dr Rajendra Prasad Sarani
Colootola Street (part)	Maulana Sawkat Ali Street
Colootola Street (part)	Anagarika Dharmapal Street
Colootola Street (part)	Acharya Brojen Sil Street
College Square	Vidyasagar Udyan
Cornwallis Street	Bidhan Sarani
Cornwallis Square	Urquhart Square
Corris Church Lane	Dr Kartick Bose Street
Cotton Street	Utkalmoni Gopabandhu Sarani
Cross Street	Jamuna Lal Bajaj Street
Dacres Lane	James Hickey Sarani

Old Name	New Name
Darga Gully	Colootola Lane & By-Lane
Dalhousie Square	Binoy Badal Dinesh Bagh
Dihi Serampur Road	Rameswar Shaw Road
Dilkhusa Street	Dr Biresh Guha Street
Dharmatala Street	Lenin Sarani
Doyehatta Street	Digamber Jain Temple Road
Dukuria Bagan Lane	Amiya Hazra Lane
Eden Hospital Road	Dr Lalit Banerjee Sarani
Elgin Road	Lala Lajpat Rai Sarani
European Asylum Lane	Comrade Andiul Halim Lane
Fancy Lane	Pannalal Bannerjee Lane
Free School Street	Mirza Ghalib Street
Galiff Street	MahatmaSisir Krishna Sarani
Gas Street	Dr M.N. Chatterjee Sarani
Gomesh Lane	Kabi Nabin Sen Lane
Government Place (part)	Marx Engels Bithi
Grey Street (Extension)	Sri Arabindra Sarani
Hanuman Gully	Synagogue Street
Haritaki Bagan Lane	Dr Dhirendra Nath Sen Sarani
Harkutta Gullee	Nabin Chand Borel Lane
Harrington Street	Ho Chi Minh Sarani
Harrison Road	Mahatma Gandhi Road
Hastings Street	Kiron Sankar Roy Road
Hayat Khan Lane	Manindra Nath Mitra Road
Hiralal Mitra Lane	Uma Charan Mitra Lane
Holwell Lane	B. Ramnath Biswas Lane

OLD AND NEW STREET NAMES

Old Name	New Name
Hunger Ford Street	Picasso Bithi
Hughes Road	Dr Ambedkar Sarani
Incinerator Road	Helen Keller Sarani
India Exchange Place	William Carey Sarani
Jackson Lane	Indra Kr. Karmani Street
Jeliatola Street	Sudhir Chatterjee Street
Kalighat Road	Manya Sardar BK Maitra Road
Kankurgachi 3rd Lane	Sachin Mitra Lane
Karaya Bazar Lane	North Range
Karaya Lane	Kazi Abdul Wadud Sarani
Karbala Road	Rafi Ahmed Kidwai Road
Kentophar Lane	Satish Ch. Mukhopadhya Sarani
Koliaghata Street	B. Terapada Mukherjee Sarani
Kyd Street	Dr Md. Isak Road
Lansdowne Road	Sarat Bose Road
Lawrance Road	Rani Rashmoni Avenue
Lindsay Street	Neli Sengupta Sarani
Little Russell Street	Nandalal Basu Sarani
Loudon Street	Dr. UN Bramachari Sarani
Lower Circular Road	Acharya J.C. Bose Road
MacCarthy Lane	Sudhir Sen Barat Lane
Macpherson Road	Amritlal Daw Road
Madan Mitra Lane (part)	Dr Bhuppa Dutta Sarani

Old Name	*New Name*
Magazine Road	Dr Rabindranath Tagore Road
Maharani Hemanta Kr. Street	Gourimata Sarani
Mangoe Lane	Surendra Mohan Ghosh Sarani
Marcus Square	Charlie Chaplin Square
Marquis Street	Mustaque Ahmed Street
Marsden Street	Paymental Street
Masjid Bari Street (part)	Akshoy Kr. Dutta Sarani
Mayo Road	Guru Nanek Sarani
Mayor Street	Bidyatan Sarani
Mechua Bazar Street	Madan Mohan Burman Street
Middleton Road	Sir William Jones Sarani
Minto Square	Bhagat Singh Udyan
Mission Row	R.N. Mukherjee Road
Mirzapur Street	Surya Sen Street
Mott Lane	Monilal Saha Lane
Muktaram Road	Rajendra Deb Sarani
Narkeldanga Lane	Dr Jagabandhu Babu Lane
Nebutala-Ka-Rasta	Pollock Street
Neogi Lane	Silpi Netai Pal Lane
Neogipukur Lane	Taltala Library Row
North Range	M. Roy Chowdhury Road
Nurmal Lohia Lane	Nurmal Lohia Street
Octerlony Road	Rani Rashmoni Avenue
Old Court House Street	Hemanta Bose Sarani
Outram Street	Nalini Guha Sarani
Pageya Putty Street	Basantial Murarka Road

OLD AND NEW STREET NAMES

Old Name	New Name
Pal Street	Jatindra Nath Bose Sarani
Panchukhansama Lane	Dr Debendra Mukherjee Row
Pattipuker	Jessore Road
Pearl Road	Dr A.M.O. Ghani Road
Phul Bagan Road	Sir Syed Ahmed Road
Portuguese Church Street	Sahid Nityananda Sarani
Princep Street (part)	Biplabi Anukul Chandra Street
Rawdon Street	Sarojini Naidu Sarani
Rash Bagan Lane	Dr Panchanan Mitra Lane
Reformatory Street	Dr Jnau Ch. Ghosh Sarani
Ripon Street	Muzaffar Ahmed Street
Robert Street	Mohin Chandra Das Sarani
Russell Street	Anandi lal Podder Sarani
Sandal Street	Moulana A.R. Malinhabad St.
Sealdah Fly over	Bidyapati Setu
Schalk Street	Durgacharan Banerjee Street
Scott Lane	Rajkumar Chakraborty Sarani
Shaikpara Lane	Ramdhan Khan Lane
Simla Street	Dr Narayan Roy Sarani
Sooterkin Street	Prafulla Sarkar Street
Soorepara	Ghosh Lane
South Road	Dr Suresh Sarkar Road
St. James Square	Santosh Mitra Square
Sukea Row	Daud Ali Dutta Sarani
Talapark Avenue	Tara Sankar Sarani
Talpukur Road	K.G. Basu Sarani
Taltala Avenue	Puran Chand Nahar Avenue

Old Name	New Name
Tari Khana Gully	Raja Debendra Narayan Lane
Theatre Road	Shakespeare Sarani
Tobin Road	Baghajotin Road
Townsend Road	Sakharam Ganesh Deuskar Sarani
Ultadanga Main Road	Bidhan Nagar Road
Upper Circular Road	Acharya Prafulla Chandra Rd.
Victoria Terrace	Gorky Sadan
Wellesley Street	Rafi Ahmed Kidwai Road
Wellesley 1st Lane	Abdul Ali Row
Wellesley 2nd Lane	A.K. Md. Siddiq Lane
Wellington Lane	Raj Kumar Bose Lane
Wellington Street	Nirmal Chandra Street
Wellington Square	Raja Subodh Mullick Square
William Lane	Dr Amal Roy Chowdhury Lane
Wood Street (part)	Dr Martin Luther King Sarani

INDEX

A

Abinash Kaviraj Street, 67, 69
Adi Banstalla Lane, 159
Ahriatola Ghat, 23, 187
Airport, 17, 18, 20, 21
Akhoy Bose Lane, 110
Albert Road, 9
Amherst Street, 9, 121, 125, 128, 129, 135, 136, 139, 144, 202, 212
Ananda Neogy Lane, 114
Anglo Indian Association, 174
Anne Monson, 178
Anthony Bagan Lane, 147
Anthony Kabial, 93
APC Road, 140, 142, 143, 145, 146, 147, 148, 202
Apne.app – Women Worldwide, 71
Armenian Church, 51, 54
Armenian Ghat, 164, 189
Armenian Street, vii, 38, 51, 52, 53, 54
Armenians, 54
Asiatic Society, 178, 196

B

B.B.D. Bagh, 9
Babu Ram Seal Lane., 136
Babulal Lane, 160
Baghbazar, viii, 15, 18, 19, 23, 92, 98, 108, 110, 111, 113, 114, 115, 166, 186, 187
Baishnab Sett 1st Lane, 82
Baithakkhana Road, 124, 125, 146
Baithakkhana., 124
Balak Dutta Lane, 44, 45
Ballar Das Street, 49
Balmukund Makkar Road, 48, 49
Banamali Sarkar Street, 97, 98, 212
Bankim Chatterjee Street, 120
barbers, 44, 50
Bawari Tola Lane, 85
BB Ganguly Street, vii, viii, xi, 15, 37, 41, 90, 93, 124, 127, 129, 133, 135, 136, 137, 139, 189
BBD Bagh, 56, 57
Beadon Street, 9, 72, 73, 79, 84, 89, 198, 212

beggars, 31, 32, 39, 88, 145, 167
Belgachia, 19, 148, 212
bheestie, 92
Bhupen Bose Avenue, 112, 192
Bidhan Nager, 19, 148
Bidhan Sarani, 9, 15, 44, 112, 189, 192, 202, 213
bidi, 39
Bipin Behari (BB) Ganguly Street, 30, 90
Biplabi Pulin Das Street, 142
Bishwakosh Lane, 111, 112
BK Paul Avenue, 94, 99
Black Hole, 63, 65
Blackburn Lane, 11, 33, 34, 35
Boi Para, viii, 118
Bonti, 28, 207
Botanical Gardens, 181, 203
Bow Bazar Street, 41
Bowbazar Orphanage Lane, 93
Brabourne Road, 51, 53, 55, 56, 58, 188, 191, 213
Braja Kumar Seth Lane, 83
Brindaban Mullick Lane, 143
brothels, 66, 70, 72, 76
Budhu Ostager Lane, 147
Burra Bazar, ix, 150, 151, 155, 156, 157, 158, 164
Burtollah Street, xi, 152, 154, 157, 159, 160
buses, v, 7, 19, 20, 74, 187

bustees, 35, 36, 40, 87, 113
Butto Kristo Paul, 85

C

Calcutta Municipal Corporation, 8, 12, 26, 82, 158
Calcutta Police, 16, 170, 174, 200, 201
Calcutta Police Museum, 200
Calcutta Rescue, iii, 113
Calcutta University, 122
Canning Street, 9, 55, 150, 192, 213
Chaatawalla Gullee, 36
Champatala 1st Bye Lane, 130
Charles Stuart. 'Hindoo Stuart', 179
Charlotte Canning, 62
China Town, 33
Chinese, 22, 33, 34, 36, 41
Chitpore Road, 9, 10, 15, 27, 186
Chitpur Bridge, xi, 87, 108, 109, 113, 117, 213
Chitpur Lock, 113
Chitpur Spur, 49
Chitteranjan (CR) Avenue, 15, 25, 116
Chitteranjan Avenue, 11
Chor Bagan, 10, 198, 213
Chor Bagan Lane, 10, 213

INDEX

Chowringhee, v, 9, 18, 110, 178, 186, 191, 194, 197, 213
Chris Smy, 1
Christian Burial Board, 174, 182
Church of our Lady of Dolours, 127
Church Street, 63, 64, 217
Circular Canal, xi, 15, 87, 108, 193, 202
Circular Railway, 18, 87, 98, 115, 187
climate, 6, 156, 176, 177, 181
Coffee House, 120
College Street, viii, 15, 29, 44, 93, 118, 119, 120, 121, 122, 123, 129, 134, 135, 136, 137, 139, 189
College Street Mall, 44, 119
College Street Market, 119
Colotolla Street, xi, 10, 25, 29, 30, 37, 38
coolies, 26, 38, 48, 49, 52, 127, 128, 151, 164, 167
Cotton Street, xi, 152, 154, 157, 160, 213
Council House Street, 60, 64
CR Avenue, 15, 27, 29, 41, 42, 43, 44, 47, 48, 50, 67, 73, 90, 108, 118, 161, 186, 188, 200

D

dadas, 170

Dalhousie Square, viii, 9, 17, 51, 56, 57, 60, 64, 65, 115, 148, 186, 214
Das Lane, 92, 120
David Ochterlony, 197
Debendra Dutta Lane, 153
Debendra Mullick Lane, 40
Derozio, 174
Dispensary Lane, 113, 114, 138
Doms, 88, 208
Dum Dum, 17, 18
Durga Charan Banerji Street, 96
Durga Charan Mitra Street, 69
Durga Charan Mukherji Street, 114
Durga Hotel, 121
Dwarkinath Tagore, 199, 200

E

East India Company, 56, 62, 115, 173, 197, 203
Eastern Railway Museum., 171
Elizabeth Jane Barwell, 178

F

Firanghee Kali Bari, 93
Fort William, 56, 58, 63, 65, 115
Francis Johnson, 63
ful jharu, 138

G

Galiff Street, 108, 109, 110, 113, 186, 214
General Clavering, 178
Giri Babu Lane, vii, 38, 41, 42
Girish Avenue, 108, 116
Girish Chandra Ghose, 72, 116
Girish Park, 18, 72, 73, 78, 89, 116, 192, 200, 202
Girish Vidya Ratna Lane, 141
Gopeswar Pal Street, 96, 97, 212
Gopi Mohan Bose Road, 93
Gorosthan Lane, 183
Great Eastern Hotel, 14, 59

H

Halder Lane, 92
hand pulled rickshaw, 22, 23
Hanspukar 1st Lane, 159
Hanumanji Lane, 154
Hari Ram Goenka Street, xi, 152, 153
Harin Bari Lane, 30, 32
Harish Skidar Path, 129
Harkutta Gullee, 133, 214
Harrison Road, 9
Hermanta Bose Sarani, 58
Hide Lane, 41
Hideram Banerji Lane., 137, 138
High Court, 62, 64
Hijeras, 137

Hindu School, 120
hospital and burial ground, 61
Hotel Himalay, 25, 26
Hotel Kolkata, 135
Hotel White House, 25
hovels, 40, 148, 153
Howrah, ix, xi, 17, 19, 23, 24, 25, 98, 148, 157, 161, 162, 163, 164, 165, 166, 167, 168, 169, 170, 172, 181, 186, 187, 188
Howrah Bridge, ix, xi, 19, 148, 157, 161, 165, 181, 186, 187, 188
Howrah Ferry Ghat, 166
Howrah Ghat, 23, 188
Howrah Railway station, 17
Hrishikesh Park, 143

I

India Exchange Place, 11, 33, 34, 35, 56, 215
Indian Museum, 196
Ismail Madan Lane, 27, 36, 43

J

Jadu Nath Dey Lane, 93
Jain Temple, 154, 202, 214
Jatindra Mohan (JM) Avenue, 67, 73, 94
Jatindra Mohan Tagore, 81
Jesus of Calcutta, v
Jewish community, 55

INDEX

JM Avenue, 78, 94, 99, 108
Job Charnock, 54, 62, 124
Job Charnock's Mausoleum, 62
John Zephaniah Holwell, 63
Jorabagan, 79
Joy Mitra Street, 67, 68

K

Kabi Raj Row, 39
Kalabagan Bustee New Road, 46
Kali Prasad Chakraborty Street, 115
Kali Shome Street, 146
Kalidas Singhee Lane, 142
Kalighat, 189, 190, 193, 204, 215
Kalkar Street, 153
Kalutola Lane, 39
Kanulal Lane, 159
Karaya Row, 183
Keshab Sen Street, 124, 140, 141, 142, 144, 145, 146, 149, 192
Kili Josiyam, 164
Krishna Dutta, 4
Kshirode Vidya Vinode Avenue, 108, 113, 116
Kumatoli, viii, 96, 97

L

Lalbazar Street, 56, 58
Lal Dighi, xi, 58, 115
Lalit Great Eastern, 59
Larkin Lane, 60
Lenin Sarani, 214
Lord Curzon, 64, 194
Lucia Palk, 176

M

Madan Baral Lane, 92
Madan Gopal Lane, 134
Madan Mohan Burman Street, 44, 46, 49, 50, 192, 216
Madho Kristo Seth Lane, 158
Madhu Gupta Lane, 129, 130
Mahatma Gandhi (MG) Road, 25
Maidan, 12, 189, 194, 195, 196, 197, 199, 210
Malinga Lane, 91, 92
Mamata Bannerjee, 64
Maratha Ditch Lane, 110
Marble Palace, 198, 199
Margaret Elizabeth Noble, 116
Masjid Bari Street, 68, 216
Maulana Saukat Ali Lane., 39
Mechua Bazar, vii, 43, 44, 119, 198, 216
Mechua wholesale fruit market, 47
Medical College and Hospital, 123

Metro, 17, 18, 25, 42, 67, 72, 73, 78, 85, 89, 90, 93, 94, 99, 112, 161, 170, 173, 188, 191, 192, 193, 195, 196, 197, 199, 200, 201, 202, 204
Metropolitan Institute, 82
MG Road, xi, 25, 26, 29, 38, 43, 47, 51, 118, 119, 121, 123, 125, 150, 151, 152, 154, 155, 160, 161, 186, 188, 191, 192, 199, 200
Minerva Theatre, 72
Mirbahar Ghat Street, 157
Missionaries of Charity, 4, 205
Mitra Lane, 46, 143, 214, 215, 217
Monsoon, 6
Mosque, 27, 32, 41, 50, 52, 71, 126, 141, 145, 146, 168, 210
Mother Theresa, 4, 5, 204, 205, 206
motor rickshaw, 8
motorised rickshaws, 22
Muchipara, 12
Muktaram Babu Lane, 46
Muktaram Babu Street, 46
Mullick Ghat Flower Market, xi, 163
Mullick Street, 53, 152
Munchi Nakibulla Lane, 145
Munshi Sadaruddin Lane, 46

N

N. Badruddin Street, 26
Nabin Chandra Borel Lane, 133
Nakhoda Mosque, 29, 30, 37, 38, 51
Nalini Sett (Seth) Road, 152
Nanda Mullick Lane, 74
Nandalal Bose Lane, 111
Nandaram Market, 160, 191, 192
Nather Bagan Lane, 86
Nather Bagan Street, 86
New CIT Road, 33, 34, 35, 40, 42, 182
Nimtola Burning Ghat, 88
Nimtola Ghat, viii, 79, 84, 85, 88, 89
Nimtola Ghat Street, 79, 84, 88, 89
Nirmal Chandra Street, xi, 15, 90, 93, 135, 137, 139, 189, 218
Nirmal Hriday, 5, 204, 205
Nirmala Shishu Bhavan, 205
Nivedita Lane, 116
NK Saha Lane., 113

O

Ochterlony Monument, 197
Old China Bazar Street, 55
Old Court House Street, 58, 216

INDEX

P

Panchanantala Lane, 137
Pandit Parashottam Roy Street, 54
Pannalal Banerji Lane, 60
Park Street, ix, 173, 174, 178, 182, 183, 197
Parsi Bagan Street, 142
Pathuria Ghat Lane, 79
Pathuriaghat, 79, 82
Pathuriaghat Street, 79
Patuatola Lane, 121
Patwar Bagan Lane, 146
pavement dwellers, 1, 90, 96, 149
Peary Das Lane, 77
Perrin's Garden, 115
Perrins Redoubt, 115
Phears Lane, 32, 39, 40
PK Tagore Street, 79, 80, 84
Pollution, 6
Portuguese Church., 53
Portuguese Street, 53
Post Office, xi, 65, 82, 156
Prasanna Kumar (PK) Tagore Street, 79
Prem Chand Borel Street, 130, 131, 133
Presidency College, 122, 123

R

Rabindra Sarani, xi, 9, 10, 11, 15, 27, 29, 30, 37, 38, 47, 49, 51, 68, 71, 72, 73, 74, 77, 79, 84, 85, 89, 95, 99, 108, 114, 116, 150, 151, 155, 158, 160, 182, 186, 198, 200, 213
Rabindranath Tagore, 162, 199, 215
ragpickers, 35, 46, 98, 121
Raj Bhavan, 64
Raja Bazar, ix, 140, 141, 145, 148
Raja Debendra Narayan Lane., 95
Raja Rajendra Mullick, 198
Rajarhat, 17
Ram Bagan, viii, 73, 75, 77
Ram Kanai Adhikari Lane, 136
Rama Krishna Lane, 114
Ram Lochan Mullick Street, 26
Ram Krishna Lane, 114
Ramakanta Bose Street, 116
Ramesh Dutta Street, 77
Ramnath Mazundar Street, 120
Rawdon Street, 173, 175, 217
recycling, 28, 29, 36, 43, 44, 46, 94
red light area, 66, 67, 75, 76, 204
RG Kar Road, 112
Richard Barwell, 178
rickshaw pullers, 6, 23
Ritu Raj Hotel, 49
river ferries, 23

River Hooghly, 15, 17, 18, 85, 87, 96, 113, 150, 161, 162, 179, 203
Rose Aylmer, 181
Rudyard Kipling, 4, 175

S

Sagar Guest House, 52
Sambhu Chatterji Street, 43, 44, 46
Sanskrit College, 120
scavengers, 35, 46, 77, 83, 121
Scavengers' Lane., 136
Scottish Cemetery, 183
Scottish Church, 58
Sealdah, 9, 17, 25, 124, 127, 140, 147, 164, 189, 217
SEED, 170
Sen Lane, 86, 134, 212, 214
Sett Bagan Gullee, 75, 79, 134
sex workers, 66, 69, 70, 71, 72, 75, 76
Shaanwalla, 126
Shakespeare Sarani, 9, 183, 199, 217
Shanti Nagar, 205
shanties, 75, 87, 108, 153
Shibpur, 24, 181, 203
Sibtala Street, 153
Sil Lane, 136, 137
Sister Nivedita, 116
Sonagachi, viii, 66, 67, 69, 70, 71, 75, 76, 133
Sonagachi Project, 70
Sophia Golborne, 176
South Park Street Cemetery, ix, 173, 174, 182, 183
Sovabazar Ferry Ghat, 98
Sovabazar Ghat, 23, 187
Sovabazar Market, 95
Sovabazar Street., 85, 99
Sri Nath Babu Lane, 32
Srimani Market, 13, 192
Srimanta Dey Lane, 91
St Andrew's Church, 56, 57, 59, 65, 183
St James' Lane, 136
St John's Church, 57, 60
St. Paul's Cathedral, 195
Station children, 170
Strand Bank Road, 87, 98
Subhas Chandra Bose, 112
Sukh Lal Jahuri Lane, 153
summer months, 6
Sun Yat Sen Street, xi, 35, 36, 41, 42
Surendra Lal Pyne Lane, 129
Surya Sen Street, 121, 122, 125, 129, 140, 147, 216
Sutanuti, 54
Syed Sally Lane, 48
Synagogue Street, 55, 214

T

Tagore Castle, 81, 84
Tagore Museum, 199
Tangra, 33
Tank Square, 57

taxi drivers, 20, 21
taxis, 21, 38, 74
tenement, 75, 76, 84, 134, 208
tenements, 75, 76
Tiretta, 32, 140, 182
Tiretta Bazar Lane, 32
Tollygunge, 17, 18, 19
Town Hall, 64
Traffic Police, 7
trafficking, 70, 71, 169
Tram Points Man, 119
trams, 6, 74, 110, 119, 161, 163, 186, 187, 189

U

Udita, 1, 6, 13, 41, 70, 140, 141, 177

V

Victoria Institution College, 148
Victoria Memorial, xi, 194, 195
Victoria Square, 9
Victoria Terrace, 9
Vidyasasgar, 138
Vivekananda Road, 15, 73, 74, 192, 200, 202

W

Walking Calcutta, iii, 2, 3
Warren Hastings, 61, 178, 179, 180
Wellesley Street, 9
William Hamilton, 62
William Jones, 178, 196, 216
winter months, 6
Writers' Building, vii, 51, 56, 57, 58, 59, 65

Y

Yogayog Bhavan, 90, 91

Z

Zakaria Street, 27
Zoffani, 61

www.ingramcontent.com/pod-product-compliance
Lightning Source LLC
Chambersburg PA
CBHW070532170426
43200CB00011B/2404